1980s

Decades of the 20th Century
Décadas del siglo XX
Decadi del XX secolo

Decades of the 20th Century
Décadas del siglo XX
Decadi del XX secolo

Nick Yapp

KÖNEMANN

This edition ©Tandem Verlag GmbH
KÖNEMANN is a trademark and an imprint of Tandem Verlag GmbH
Photographs ©2001 Getty Images

This book was produced by Getty Images
Unique House, 21–31 Woodfield Road, London W9 2BA

For KÖNEMANN:
Managing editor: Sally Bald
Project editors: Lucile Bas, Meike Hilbring

For Getty Images: Picture editor: Ali Khoja
Art director: Michael Rand Editor: Richard Collins
Design: Tea McAleer Proof reader: Liz Ihre

© 2004 for the trilingual edition English, Spanish and Italian:
Tandem Verlag GmbH
KÖNEMANN is a trademark and an imprint of Tandem Verlag GmbH
Spanish translation: Laura Sales Gutiérrez for LocTeam, S. L., Barcelona
Italian translation: Maurizio Siliato for LocTeam, S. L., Barcelona
Text editing and typesetting: LocTeam, S. L., Barcelona

Printed in China

ISBN 3-8331-1152-6

10 9 8 7 6 5 4 3
X IX VIII VII VI V IV III II I

Frontispiece: The spirit of the age. A Salvadorean soldier runs for cover
during an exchange of gunfire with FMLN guerrillas in the city of Apopa.
Civil war raged across El Salvador throughout the 1980s.

Frontispicio: El espíritu de la época. Un soldado salvadoreño corre para
refugiarse durante un tiroteo con las guerrillas del FMLN en la ciudad de
Apopa. La guerra civil asoló El Salvador a lo largo de los años ochenta.

Frontespizio: Lo spirito dell'epoca. Un soldato salvadoregno corre al riparo
durante uno scontro a fuoco con le guerriglie dell'FMLN nella città di Apopa.
La guerra civile imperversò su El Salvador durante l'intero decennio.

Contents / Contenido / Sommario

Introduction

True to the formula recommended for modern movie plots, the 20th century reached crisis point as it approached its end. The tension between haves and have-nots, between power and the people, between labour and capital increased dramatically. The old tools of negotiation and compromise seemed inadequate for the job in hand – driving the world forward to new economies, new alliances, new social structures. Unemployment became a condition rather than a temporary misfortune for millions. Democracy became the servant rather than the basis of government. The lack of personal freedom under Communism became overwhelmingly more important than the security the system offered.

The result was a series of explosions – some of mighty proportions. There were wars of old-fashioned colonial-style simplicity (in the Falklands, Grenada, Libya, Zimbabwe) and of new complexity (in the Lebanon, Afghanistan, Angola). An epidemic of riots and revolutions brought down governments in Haiti, Poland, El Salvador, the Philippines and Panama; and tested the mettle of others in India, Chile, Britain, South Africa, France and South Korea. Most of the satellite governments of Eastern Europe managed to maintain their trembling hold on a withering authority into the 1990s.

There were new kids on the block, new faces in new places. The yuppie emerged as the Bright Young Thing of the Eighties – proud, ambitious, hard working but myopic. New Man washed up, fed his babies, cleaned the house and battled to erase (or at least limit) the worst side effects of his testosterone. Women invaded what had formerly been 'men only' arenas. In September 1983 the United States selected its first black Miss America.

And the world continued to crash its gears, never certain whether it wished to go forward or backwards. The last Playboy club closed in 1988. Texas voted to cease teaching the theory of evolution in 1984. Capital punishment returned to many American states. The first female astronauts came on stream. The Jeep made a comeback. The stealth bomber made its sinister debut. A solar-powered aircraft flew the Channel. A baboon's heart was implanted in a baby. The world stock markets soared in August 1987 and crashed two months later.

There were gluts of oil and desperate shortages of food. The worst drought for fifty years parched much of the world's surface in 1988. Pollution established itself as a major player on the world scene, with the horrors of Chernobyl and Bhopal well to the fore. The worst ever air disaster occurred on Mount Osutaka, Japan, in August 1985. An earthquake devastated Armenia in December 1988.

Through it all shone the hope and enthusiasm of the human race – ever-ingenious, ever-inventive, ever-industrious... but perhaps for a brief moment losing some of its concern for its fellows and its planet.

Introducción

Como si se tratara de un guión cinematográfico adaptado a la fórmula estructural recomendada actualmente, el siglo XX vivió un momento de crisis precisamente cuando se acercaba a su fin. Las tensiones aumentaron espectacularmente: entre ricos y pobres, entre el poder y el pueblo, entre el trabajo y el capital. Los antiguos instrumentos de negociación y acuerdo parecían inadecuados para el propósito de la década: hacer avanzar el mundo hacia nuevas economías, nuevas alianzas y nuevas estructuras sociales. Para millones de personas, el desempleo dejó de ser un infortunio pasajero y se convirtió en un estado permanente. La democracia pasó a estar al servicio del gobierno, en vez de ocupar un lugar en sus mismos fundamentos. La falta de libertad personal en los países comunistas cobró mucha más importancia que la seguridad que ofrecía el sistema.

Como consecuencia, se produjeron varios estallidos de violencia, algunos de inmensas proporciones. Estallaron guerras motivadas por visiones antiguas y simplistas, propias de la época colonial (en las islas Malvinas, Granada, Libia y Zimbaue) y otras que revestían una nueva complejidad (en el Líbano, Afganistán o Angola). Una epidemia de disturbios y revoluciones derrocó los gobiernos de Haití, Polonia, El Salvador, Filipinas y Panamá, y puso a prueba la solidez de otros: India, Chile, Gran Bretaña, Sudáfrica, Francia y Corea del Sur. La mayoría de los gobiernos satélites de Europa del Este consiguieron mantener su férrea autoridad, aunque con pulso tembloroso, hasta los años noventa.

Hubo nuevos inquilinos en el mundo, nuevas caras en nuevos destinos. Surgió la figura del *yuppy*, la nueva gran promesa de los años ochenta: orgulloso, ambicioso y trabajador incansable, aunque miope en su visión del mundo. También apareció en escena un hombre nuevo, que lavaba los platos, daba de comer a sus hijos, limpiaba la casa y luchaba para borrar, o como mínimo reducir, los peores efectos secundarios de la testosterona. Las mujeres invadieron territorios reservados hasta entonces a los hombres. En septiembre de 1983, Estados Unidos eligió a la primera Miss América negra.

Y el mundo continuaba girando, sin acabar de decidir hacia dónde debía caminar: atrás o adelante. El último club Playboy cerró sus puertas en 1988. En 1984, Texas aprobó por votación popular dejar de enseñar en las escuelas la teoría de la evolución. La pena de muerte se reinstauró en muchos estados de Estados Unidos. Surgieron las primeras astronautas. El *jeep* se volvió a poner de moda. El bombardero invisible hizo su siniestro debut. Un avión con energía solar sobrevoló el canal de La Mancha y se trasplantó un corazón de babuino a un bebé. Las Bolsas de todo el mundo se dispararon en agosto de 1987 y se desplomaron dos meses después.

Hubo exceso de oferta de petróleo y terribles carencias de alimentos. La peor sequía en cincuenta años resecó gran parte de la superficie mundial en 1988. Por otra parte, la contaminación atmosférica se consolidó como un factor determinante en el escenario mundial, con las catástrofes de Chernóbil y Bhopal en primera plana de la actualidad. En agosto de 1985 se produjo el peor accidente aéreo de la historia en el monte Osutaka, Japón. Un terremoto asoló Armenia en diciembre de 1988.

Los años ochenta fueron la década de la esperanza y el entusiasmo. La humanidad parecía más ingeniosa, más inventiva y más trabajadora que nunca. Con todo, quizá por un breve instante, dejó de preocuparse por el bienestar de sus semejantes y de su planeta.

Introduzione

Fedele alla formula raccomandata per le ambientazioni del cinema moderno, il XX secolo giunse a un punto critico mentre volgeva al suo termine. La tensione tra gli abbienti e i meno abbienti, tra il potere e le persone, tra il lavoro e il capitale aumentò in maniera drammatica. I vecchi strumenti utilizzati per negoziare ed arrivare a dei compromessi sembravano inadeguati per il compito in questione: condurre il mondo verso nuove economie, nuove alleanze, nuove strutture sociali. Per milioni di persone la disoccupazione divenne uno stato cronico piuttosto che una sventura passeggera. Anziché costituirne la base, la democrazia si mise al servizio del governo. La mancanza di libertà personale sotto il regime comunista divenne enormemente più importante della sicurezza offerta dal sistema.

Tutto ciò scaturì in una serie di esplosioni, alcune delle quali di proporzioni enormi. Ci furono delle guerre improntate a dei semplici modelli di vecchio stampo colonialistico (nelle Falkland, a Grenada, in Libia, nello Zimbabwe) ed altre caratterizzate da una nuova complessità (nel Libano, in Afghanistan, in Angola). Un'epidemia di rivolte e di rivoluzioni fece cadere i governi di Haiti, della Polonia, di El Salvador, delle Filippine e di Panama, e mise alla prova quelli di India, Cile, Gran Bretagna, Sud Africa, Francia e Corea del Sud. Nonostante la loro autorità ormai in declino, la maggior parte dei governi satellite dell'Europa dell'Est riuscì a mantenere il controllo sulle masse fino agli inizi degli anni Novanta.

Stava emergendo una nuova generazione, fatta di volti nuovi e nuovi scenari. Negli anni Ottanta il nuovo modello da seguire sono gli yuppie: orgogliosi, ambiziosi, alacri lavoratori ma privi di lungimiranza. Il Nuovo Uomo lavava i piatti, dava da mangiare ai bambini, puliva la casa e faceva di tutto per eliminare (o quantomeno limitare) gli effetti collaterali meno gradevoli del suo machismo. Le donne invasero quei territori che fino allora erano stati riservati solamente agli uomini. Nel settembre 1983 gli Stati Uniti elessero la prima Miss America di colore.

Nel frattempo, il mondo continuava a premere sull'acceleratore, senza essere mai troppo sicuro di voler avanzare o andare indietro. L'ultimo club Playboy chiuse i battenti nel 1988. In Texas si votò per abolire l'insegnamento della teoria evolutiva nel 1984. La pena di morte venne ripristinata in molti stati americani. Si iniziarono a vedere le prime astronaute. La Jeep ritornò sul mercato. Il bombardiere invisibile fece il suo tragico debutto mentre un aereo ad energia solare riusciva a sorvolare la Manica. Il cuore di un babbuino venne trapiantato a un bambino. I mercati borsistici di tutto il mondo andarono alle stelle nell'agosto 1987 prima del loro strepitoso crollo, due mesi più tardi.

C'era una sovrabbondanza di petrolio e una disperata penuria di cibo. Nel 1988 la peggiore siccità verificatasi negli ultimi cinquant'anni fece inaridire gran parte della superficie mondiale. L'inquinamento si configurò come protagonista principale della scena mondiale, portando alla ribalta le raccapriccianti immagini di Chernobyl e di Bhopal. Il peggior disastro aereo accadde sul Monte Osutaka, in Giappone, nell'agosto del 1985. Un terremoto devastò l'Armenia nel dicembre del 1988. Il decennio fu comunque contrassegnato dalla speranza e l'entusiasmo di una razza umana, sempre più ingegnosa, creativa e operosa… ma che a volte trascurava i suoi simili e il suo pianeta.

1. Movers and shakers
Líderes y agitadores
Progressisti e agitatori

Heading for re-election. A Churchillian portrait of Margaret Thatcher, March 1983. Two months later the Iron Lady won a second term in office and intensified her campaign to change the face of Britain.

En el camino hacia la reelección. Retrato con tintes churchillianos de Margaret Thatcher, marzo de 1983. Dos meses después, la Dama de Hierro consiguió continuar en el poder durante un segundo mandato e intensificó su campaña para cambiar la fisonomía de Gran Bretaña.

Verso la rielezione. Un ritratto dai toni churcilliani di Margaret Thatcher, marzo 1983. Due mesi dopo la Lady di Ferro conquistò la sua seconda legislatura al potere e intensificò la propria campagna per cambiare il volto della Gran Bretagna.

1. Movers and shakers
Líderes y agitadores
Progressisti e agitatori

An almost totally new cast was assembled for the dramas of the 1980s. Thatcher and the Ayatollah Khomeini had both come to power in 1979, but Reagan and Bush, Mugabe, Jaruzelski and Walesa, Gorbachev, Mitterrand and Kohl were all new on the scene. Together, they and dozens of others presided over a decade that saw the end of the world that had been constructed after the Second World War, and the beginning of political post-modernism.

They set about their appointed tasks with single-minded gusto that polarised the political scene. What they had to offer were new solutions directed at new problems – global communication, market economies, managing nuclear waste – rather than the eternal problems of poverty, disease, famine and oppression.

They shook much of the world by the scruff of its neck, administering the last rites to traditional trade unionism, to one-nation conservatism, to the Berlin Wall. They initiated the later collapse of the Soviet Empire. When, however, the dust settled a decade or so later, the world was recognisably the same – warts and all.

Los dramas de los años ochenta renovaron sus protagonistas casi en su totalidad. Thatcher y el ayatolá Jomeini ya habían llegado al poder en 1979, pero Reagan y Bush, Mugabe, Jaruzelski y Walesa, Gorbachov, Mitterrand y Kohl eran nuevos en la escena. Todos ellos, junto a varias decenas más de dirigentes políticos, presidieron la década que puso fin al mundo erigido tras la Segunda Guerra Mundial y dio paso a los primeros tiempos de la posmodernidad política.

Los nuevos dirigentes emprendieron las tareas encomendadas con un entusiasmo irrefrenable que polorarizó el escenario político mundial. Su papel consistía en ofrecer soluciones nuevas para problemas nuevos –comunicación global, economías de mercado, gestión de los residuos nucleares– en lugar de resolver los eternos problemas de la humanidad: pobreza, enfermedad, hambre y represión.

Sus políticas sacudieron buena parte del mundo y administraron la ultima unción al sindicalismo tradicional, al conservadurismo de base nacional y al Muro de Berlín. Iniciaron también el posterior hundimiento del imperio soviético. Pero cuando aproximadamente una década más tarde pasó la tormenta, se hizo evidente que el mundo seguía siendo el mismo y que obviamente conservaba todos los defectos heredados.

A presenziare i drammatici avvenimenti degli anni Ottanta ci fu un gruppo di attori politici quasi del tutto nuovi. A parte la Thatcher e l'Ayatollah Khomeini, entrambi saliti al potere nel 1979, Reagan e Bush, Mugabe, Jaruzelski e Walesa, Gorbaciov, Mitterrand e Kohl erano volti nuovi della scena politica. Tutti costoro, insieme a decine di altri dirigenti, furono alla guida di un decennio che vide la fine di quel mondo costruito dopo la Seconda guerra mondiale e l'inizio del post-modernismo politico.

Questi capi di governo svolsero i loro compiti con un modo di operare del tutto personale, spaccando in due la scena politica. Dovevano proporre nuove soluzioni per nuovi problemi – comunicazioni globali, economie di mercato, gestione e smaltimento delle scorie nucleari – piuttosto che per i problemi di sempre: povertà, malattie, penuria e oppressione.

Presero il mondo per la collottola e gli diedero una bella scossa, celebrando gli ultimi riti del sindacalismo tradizionale, del conservatorismo della nazione, del Muro di Berlino. Avviarono il futuro crollo dell'Impero Sovietico. Ad ogni modo, una volta ristabilitasi la calma, a distanza più o meno di un decennio, poterono constatare che il mondo era rimasto uguale – sotto ogni aspetto.

Mikhail Gorbachev of the Soviet Union (left) and Ronald Reagan of the United States meet beneath their respective flags at the Geneva Summit, 19 November 1985. Little was achieved beyond reducing international tension.

Mijaíl Gorbachov, presidente de la Unión Soviética (izquierda), y el dirigente estadounidense Ronald Reagan se encuentran bajo sus banderas respectivas en la Cumbre de Ginebra, el 19 de noviembre de 1985. La reunión no arrojó resultados concretos, pero se consiguió reducir la tensión internacional.

Il presidente dell'Unione Sovietica Mikhail Gorbaciov (a sinistra) e il presidente americano Ronald Reagan si incontrano sotto le loro rispettive bandiere al Summit di Ginevra, 19 novembre 1985. L'incontro diede pochi risultati, ma permise di ridurre la tensione internazionale.

WHITE HOUSE/BLACK STAR/COLORIFIC!

(Opposite) The balloonatic. Ronald Reagan peeps through a sea of balloons in Iowa during his 1984 presidential campaign. (Above) Not her usual dummy. Nancy Reagan (right), the First Lady, clowns her way through cabaret time at the annual Congressional barbecue held in the Diplomatic Reception Room of the White House, Washington, DC.

(Página anterior) Jugando con globos. Ronald Reagan asoma la cabeza entre un mar de globos en un acto de la campaña presidencial celebrado en Iowa en 1984. (Arriba) Otra clase de payasadas. Nancy Reagan (derecha), primera dama estadounidense, hace el payaso en la barbacoa tradicional del Congreso de Estados Unidos, celebrada en la sala de recepción diplomática de la Casa Blanca en Washington D. C.

(Pagina a fianco) Con la testa nel pallone. Ronald Reagan guarda attraverso un mare di palloncini durante la sua campagna presidenziale del 1984, Iowa. (In alto) Più pagliaccesca del solito, la first lady Nancy Reagan (a destra) scherza con i clown durante lo spettacolo dell'annuale barbecue del Congresso, svoltosi presso la sala di ricezione diplomatica della Casa Bianca, Washington, DC.

(Opposite) Step aside Blue Eyes. Reagan cuts in on Frank Sinatra to dance with his wife Nancy in the White House East Room, 9 February 1981. (Above) Reagan with President-elect George Bush (right), 20 January 1989.

(Página anterior) Aparta, Sinatra. Reagan le pide a Frank Sinatra que le permita bailar con su esposa Nancy en la East Room de la Casa Blanca, el 9 de febrero de 1981. (Arriba) Reagan con el presidente electo George Bush (derecha), el 20 de enero de 1989.

(Pagina a fianco) Fatti da parte, Frankie. Reagan interrompe Frank Sinatra per ballare con sua moglie Nancy nella East Room della Casa Bianca, 9 febbraio 1981. (In alto) Reagan con il neo-eletto presidente George Bush (a destra), 20 gennaio 1989.

RICK FRIEDMAN/BLACK STAR/COLORIFIC!

(Above and opposite) Moment of relief. George Bush and his wife Barbara at the Republican Party National Convention, New Orleans, 18 August 1988. In 1980 Bush had contested the Republican presidential nomination with Reagan.

(Arriba y página siguiente) Un pequeño descanso. George Bush y su esposa Barbara en la Convención Nacional del Partido Republicano, Nueva Orleans, 18 de agosto de 1988. En 1980 Bush se disputó con Reagan la candidatura presidencial por el Partido Republicano.

(In alto e nella pagina a fianco) Momento di sollievo. George Bush e la moglie Barbara alla Convenzione nazionale del Partito Repubblicano, New Orleans, 18 agosto 1988. Nel 1980 Bush aveva conteso a Reagan la nomina repubblicana per le elezioni presidenziali.

RICK FRIEDMAN/BLACK STAR/COLORIFIC!

For the next eight years he was the best of Vice-Presidents, loyal and uncharismatic, playing an important role in forming and implementing foreign policy, and successfully skating over the thin ice of Irangate.

Durante los ocho años siguientes fue el mejor de los vicepresidentes, leal y poco carismático, desempeñó un papel fundamental en la elaboración y la aplicación de la política exterior, y consiguió salir airoso del espinoso asunto Irangate.

Negli otto anni successivi Bush fu il migliore dei vicepresidenti, fedele e privo di carisma. Svolse un ruolo di rilevo nella preparazione ed attuazione della politica estera, e schivò abilmente lo scandalo dell'Irangate.

KEYSTONE/HULTON|ARCHIVE

Bad days at Brighton. (Above) At the 1985 Tory Party Conference, Margaret Thatcher is perhaps haunted by memories of the previous year's bombing. (Opposite) Neil Kinnock's sad imitation of King Canute, 2 October 1983.

Un mal día en Brighton. (Arriba) En el Congreso del Partido Conservador de 1985, Margaret Thatcher parece perseguida por el recuerdo del atentado perpetrado el año anterior. (Página siguiente) Neil Kinnock en una mala imitación del rey Canuto, 2 de octubre de 1983.

Tempi brutti a Brighton. (In alto) Al congresso del Partito conservatore del 1985, Margaret Thatcher viene forse tormentata dal ricordo dell'attentato dell'anno precedente. (Pagina a fianco) Neil Kinnock imita goffamente il Re Canuto, 2 ottobre 1983.

Underground power. Chancellor Helmut Kohl of West Germany emerges from a visit to the coalface of a mine.

Energía subterránea. El canciller de la República Federal de Alemania Helmut Kohl sale al exterior tras una visita al frente de explotación de una mina de carbón.

Potere sotterraneo. Il cancelliere della Germania Ovest Helmut Kohl, durante una visita a una miniera di carbone, emerge dal fronte di abbattimento.

Underwater deterrent. President François Mitterrand attends the inauguration of the French nuclear submarine *Inflexible*, Brest, 1985.

Disuasión submarina. El presidente François Mitterrand asiste a la inauguración del submarino nuclear francés *Inflexible* en Brest, 1985.

Deterrente sottomarino. Il presidente François Mitterrand prende parte all'inaugurazione del sottomarino nucleare francese *Inflexible*, Brest, 1985.

BOCCON GIBBOD/BLACK STAR/COLORIFIC!

WHITE HOUSE/HULTON|ARCHIVE

'Honey, I forgot to duck.' The immediate aftermath of John Hinckley Jnr's assassination attempt on President Reagan, outside the Washington Hilton Hotel, 30 March 1981. Reagan was wounded in the left lung.

"Cariño, me olvidé de agacharme." Instantánea tomada inmediatamente después del intento de asesinato del presidente estadounidense Ronald Reagan a cargo de John Hinckley Junior delante del hotel Hilton de Washington el 30 de marzo de 1981. Reagan resultó herido en el pulmón izquierdo.

"Tesoro, ho dimenticato di abbassarmi". I momenti successivi al tentato omicidio da parte di John Hinckley Junior del presidente Reagan, davanti all'Hotel Hilton di Washington, 30 marzo 1981. Reagan rimase ferito al polmone sinistro.

REUTERS/HULTON|ARCHIVE

Pope John Paul II is lifted from his 'popemobile' after being shot in the stomach by Mehmet Ali Agca, St Peter's Square, Rome, 13 May 1981. Eighteen months later, the Pope visited Ali Agca in gaol to offer his forgiveness.

Juan Pablo II recibe ayuda para salir del "papamóvil" después de que Mehmet Ali Agca le disparara en el vientre en la plaza de San Pedro de Roma el 13 de mayo de 1981. Dieciocho meses después, el Papa visitó a Ali Agca en la cárcel en señal de perdón.

Papa Giovanni Paolo II viene sollevato dalla papamobile dopo essere stato ferito allo stomaco dagli spari di Mehmet Ali Agca, in piazza San Pietro, Roma, 13 maggio 1981. Diciotto mesi dopo, il Papa visitò Ali Agca in prigione per concedergli il perdono.

President Anwar Sadat of Egypt, 13 February 1981. Three years earlier, he and Menachem Begin of Israel had jointly received the Nobel Peace Prize.

El presidente egipcio Anwar Sadat, 13 de febrero de 1981. Tres años antes había recibido conjuntamente con el israelí Menachem Begin el premio Nobel de la Paz.

Il presidente egiziano Anwar Sadat, 13 febbraio 1981. Tre anni prima, lui e l'allora primo ministro israeliano Menachem Begin avevano vinto ex aequo il premio Nobel per la pace.

NAKRAM AL AKHBAR/LIAISON AGENCY

Sadat is assassinated by Islamic fundamentalist gunmen at the Annual Commemorative
Military Parade for the 1973 Arab–Israeli war, Cairo, 6 October 1981. A number of
Arab nations openly applauded his assassination.

Sadat fue asesinado por fundamentalistas islámicos en el desfile militar anual celebrado
en El Cairo, en conmemoración de la guerra árabe israelí de 1973 el 6 de octubre de
1981. Varios estados árabes aplaudieron abiertamente el atentado.

Il Cairo, 6 ottobre 1981. Sadat fu assassinato da un fondamentalista islamico in
occasione dell'annuale parata militare per commemorare la guerra arabo-israeliana
del Kippur del 1973. Varie nazioni arabe approvarono apertamente il suo assassinio.

VOLKER CORELL/BLACK STAR/COLORIFIC!

After clashes between Sikhs and Hindus in Amritsar in June 1984, the Indian Prime Minister Indira Gandhi (above) ordered troops to storm the Golden Temple, the holiest of Sikh shrines. Four months later, Mrs Gandhi was assassinated by her own bodyguards.

Después de los enfrentamientos entre sijs e hindúes en Amritsar en junio de 1984, la primera ministra india Indira Gandhi (arriba) ordenó al ejército que asaltara el Templo Dorado, el lugar sagrado más importante para los sijs. Cuatro meses después, Indira Gandhi fue asesinada por sus propios guardaespaldas.

Dopo gli scontri tra i sikh e gli indù, verificatisi ad Amritsar nel giugno 1984, il primo ministro indiano Indira Gandhi (in alto) ordinò di prendere d'assalto il Tempio d'Oro, il più sacro dei santuari sikh. Quattro mesi dopo, Indira Gandhi fu assassinata dalle sue stesse guardie del corpo.

Rajiv Gandhi
(centre, in white hat)
watches over the
funeral pyre
of his mother,
Indira Gandhi,
November 1984.

Rajiv Gandhi
(centro, con un
bonete blanco)
contempla la pira
funeraria de su
madre, Indira
Gandhi, en
noviembre
de 1984.

Rajiv Gandhi (al
centro, con il képi
bianco) veglia sulla
pira funeraria della
madre, Indira
Gandhi, novembre
1984.

COLORIFIC!

Prompting the witness… Colonel Oliver North listens to his
counsel during the Iran-Contra hearings before the Joint House of
Representatives and Senate Committee, Washington, DC, May 1987.

Testigo con apuntador… El coronel Oliver North en una comparecencia
del caso Irán-Contra ante la comisión interparlamentaria de la Cámara
de Representantes y del Senado, Washington D. C., mayo de 1987.

Suggerimento al testimone… Il colonnello Oliver North ascolta
il suo avvocato durante l'udienza del caso Iran-Contra davanti alla
commissione interparlamentare della Camera dei rappresentanti e
del Senato, Washington DC, maggio 1987.

Silent witness. The Ayatollah Khomeini of Iran contemplates the future. He ruled Iran from 1979 to 1989.

Testigo silencioso. El ayatolá Jomeini reflexiona sobre el futuro. Gobernó Irán de 1979 a 1989.

Testimone silenzioso. Il leader iraniano Ayatollah Khomeini contempla il futuro. Governò l'Iran dal 1979 al 1989.

MICHAEL COYNE/BLACK STAR/COLORIFIC!

FRANCOIS LEHR/SIPA PRESS

Colonel Muammar Gaddafi attends celebrations of the 18th anniversary of
the Republic of Libya, September 1987. In 1969 he had led the Free Officers
Movement which overthrew the former ruler, King Idris.

El coronel Muammar el Gaddafi en la celebración del decimoctavo aniversario de
la República de Libia, en septiembre de 1987. En 1969 lideró el Grupo de Oficiales
Libres, que derrocó al antiguo dirigente del país, el rey Idris.

Il colonnello Muammar Gheddafi partecipa alle celebrazioni del 18° anniversario
della Repubblica libica, settembre 1987. Nel 1969 era stato a capo del movimento
libico dei Liberi Ufficiali che depose l'allora governante re Idris I.

President Saddam
Hussein visits the
front during the
Iran–Iraq war,
21 March 1988.
Millions had already
died in the war
which began in
September 1981.

El presidente de Irak
Sadam Husein visita
el frente durante la
guerra entre Irán e
Irak, 21 de marzo
de 1988. El
conflicto, iniciado
en septiembre de
1981, ya había
causado millones
de víctimas.

Il presidente Saddam
Hussein visita il
fronte durante la
guerra tra l'Iran
e l'Iraq, 21 marzo
1988. Il conflitto,
scoppiato nel
settembre del 1981,
aveva già mietuto
milioni di vittime.

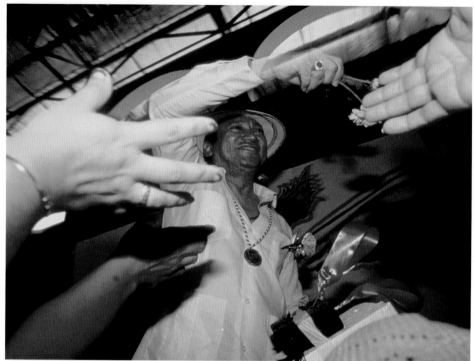

CHRISTOPHER MORRIS/BLACK STAR/COLORIFIC!

Temporary success. President Manuel Noriega celebrates the failure of a coup attempt, Panama City, October 1989. The celebrations did not last long. Noriega was finally ousted eight weeks later.

Éxito temporal. El presidente Manuel Noriega celebra el fracaso de un golpe de estado en Panamá en octubre de 1989. La celebración no duró demasiado: Noriega fue derrocado ocho semanas después.

Successo temporaneo. Il presidente Manuel Noriega festeggia il tentativo fallito di un colpo di stato, a Panama, ottobre 1989. I festeggiamenti non durarono a lungo. Otto anni dopo Noriega venne definitivamente spodestato.

Temporary bandage. General Augusto Pinochet nurses his left hand, injured during an assassination attempt, 22 September 1986.

Vendaje temporal. El general Augusto Pinochet se protege la mano izquierda, tras ser herido en un intento de asesinato el 22 de septiembre de 1986.

Fasciatura temporanea. Il generale Augusto Pinochet si cura la mano sinistra, rimasta ferita in occasione del mancato attentato, 22 settembre 1986.

ERIK DE CASTRO/REUTERS/HULTON|ARCHIVE

'Come on baby light my fire…': Imelda Marcos woos and wows her
dictatorial husband, President Ferdinand Marcos, during an election
campaign, Manila, 11 January 1986.

"Come on baby light my fire…": Imelda Marcos corteja y seduce a su
esposo, el dictador y presidente de Filipinas Ferdinand Marcos, durante
un acto electoral en Manila, el 11 de enero de 1986.

"Come on baby light my fire…": Imelda Marcos osserva entusiasta e con
sguardo ammiccante suo marito, il dittatore Ferdinando Marcos, durante
un momento della campagna elettorale, Manila, 11 gennaio 1986.

President P W Botha lays it down big time on a marimba after opening a training and work centre, Crossroads township, South Africa, 26 August 1988.

El presidente P. W. Botha impone su ley a ritmo de marimba, después de inaugurar un centro de formación y empleo en el distrito segregado de Crossroads, Sudáfrica, el 26 de agosto de 1988.

Il presidente P.W. Botha si diverte a suonare la marimba dopo aver inaugurato un centro formativo-occupazionale nella township sudafricana di Crossroads, 26 agosto 1988.

ULLI MICHEL/REUTERS/HULTON|ARCHIVE

2. Conflict
Conflictos
Conflitti

Sisters in arms. Members of the Iranian militia march through the streets of Tehran to celebrate the Day of the Woman, 24 March 1984. The war between Iran and Iraq was at its height at this time.

Hermanas de armas. Miembros de la milicia iraní desfilan por las calles de Teherán para celebrar el Día de la Mujer, el 24 de marzo de 1984. Era la etapa más cruda de la guerra entre Irán e Irak.

Sorelle d'armi. Membri della milizia iraniana marciano per le strade di Teheran per celebrare la Giornata della Donna, 24 marzo 1984. All'epoca, la guerra tra l'Iran e l'Iraq era all'apice.

2. Conflict
Conflictos
Conflitti

Forty years on from the Second World War, the world managed to avoid another global conflict. Fighting was local, rather than on the grand scale. There were wars of liberation, of revolution, of colonial greed, and between unhappy neighbours. There were bombing raids and instances of armed intervention – notably by the United States.

The Soviet Union spent lives and resources in an ultimately unsuccessful attempt to save Afghanistan from the encroaching *mujahedin*; Britain reverted to 19th-century patterns of behaviour when a handful of Argentinian scientists and soldiers landed in South Georgia; Iran and Iraq spent most of the decade in bitter dispute. There were armed insurrections in Colombia, Nicaragua, El Salvador, Chile, the Philippines, Haiti and Panama. The civil war in Angola dragged on throughout the decade. Riots erupted in South Africa, South Korea, south London, Northern Ireland and France.

In a decade of chilly catchphrases – 'second cold war', 'Soviet and US neo-colonial expansion', 'evil empire', 'ideological warfare', 'nuclear stockpiling' – it was a mercy that the anticipated holocaust between East and West did not materialise.

Cuarenta años después de la Segunda Guerra Mundial, el mundo consiguió evitar otro conflicto global. En los años ochenta se disputaron conflictos locales, más que a gran escala. Estallaron guerras de liberación, revolucionarias, motivadas por la codicia colonial y por las rivalidades entre vecinos insatisfechos. Hubo bombardeos aéreos y muestras de intervención armada, especialmente a cargo de Estados Unidos.

La Unión Soviética consumió vidas humanas y recursos materiales en el intento finalmente fallido de salvar Afganistán de la invasión de los muyahidin; Gran Bretaña recuperó modelos de conducta del siglo XIX cuando un puñado de científicos y soldados argentinos aterrizaron en las islas Georgias del Sur, e Irán e Irak mantuvieron durante la mayor parte de la década una enconada disputa. Se produjeron insurrecciones armadas en Colombia, Nicaragua, El Salvador, Chile, Filipinas, Haití y Panamá. La guerra civil de Angola se prolongó durante toda la década. Se vivieron también disturbios en Sudáfrica, Corea del Sur, el sur de Londres, Irlanda del Norte y Francia.

En una década de eslóganes escalofriantes –"segunda guerra fría", "expasión neocolonial soviética y estadounidense", "imperio del mal", "guerra ideológica", "arsenal nuclear"– fue una gran suerte que el vaticinado holocausto entre Oriente y Occidente no llegara a materializarse.

Quarant'anni dopo la Seconda guerra mondiale, il mondo era riuscito ad evitare lo scoppio di un altro conflitto mondiale. I combattimenti si svolsero in ambito locale, e non su larga scala. Vi furono guerre di liberazione, di stampo rivoluzionario, guerre mosse dalla brama colonialistica, e dai bellicosi rapporti tra paesi vicini. Non mancarono i bombardamenti aerei e i casi di intervento delle forze armate – in particolare da parte degli Stati Uniti.

L'Unione Sovietica perse molte vite e impiegò varie risorse militari in un ultimo e vano tentativo di salvare l'Afghanistan dall'occupazione dei mujaheddin; la Gran Bretagna rispose allo sbarco di una manciata di scienziati e soldati argentini in Georgia del Sud utilizzando dei metodi degni del XIX secolo; l'Iran e l'Iraq trascorsero quasi l'intero decennio impegnati in un conflitto spietato. Vi furono insurrezioni armate in Colombia, Nicaragua, El Salvador, Cile, Filippine, Haiti e Panama. La guerra civile in Angola si protrasse per tutto il decennio. Scoppiarono delle rivolte in Sud Africa, Corea del Sud, nella zona sud di Londra, nell'Irlanda del Nord e in Francia.

In una decade di slogan raggelanti – "seconda guerra fredda", "espansione neo-coloniale russa ed americana", "impero del male", "guerra ideologica", "armamento nucleare" – è stata una fortuna che l'atteso olocausto tra l'Est e l'Ovest non si sia materializzato.

STRINGER/REUTERS/HULTON|ARCHIVO

Protection. A Muslim *mullah* (left) and a member of the Iranian Revolutionary Guard visit the battle zone near Oshnoviyeh in north-west Iran, 8 August 1988. Iran repeatedly claimed that the Iraqis were using chemical weapons.

Protección. Un *mulá* musulmán (izquierda) y un miembro de la Guardia Revolucionaria Iraní visitan el campo de batalla próximo a Oshnoviyeh, en el noroeste de Irán, el 8 de agosto de 1988. Irán había afirmado repetidas veces que los iraquíes utilizaban armas químicas.

Protezione. Un mullah islamico (a sinistra) e un membro della Guardia rivoluzionaria iraniana visitano il campo di battaglia vicino Oshnoviyeh nel nord-ovest dell'Iran, 8 agosto 1988. L'Iran ha più volte sostenuto che gli iracheni stessero usando armi chimiche.

OZTURK/SIPA PRESS

Destruction. Two of the 5,000 who died when Iraqi troops used chemical weapons to bombard a Kurdish village in a region occupied by Iran. The Iran–Iraq war was the most destructive of the decade.

Destrucción. Dos de las cinco mil víctimas que perecieron cuando el ejército iraquí atacó con armas químicas un pueblo kurdo situado en una región ocupada por Irán. La guerra entre Irán e Irak fue la más destructiva de la década.

Distruzione. Due delle 5.000 vittime che persero la vita quando le truppe irachene usarono armi chimiche per bombardare un villaggio curdo in una regione occupata dall'Iran. Il conflitto Iran–Iraq fu il più disastroso del decennio.

ALFRED/LIAISON AGENCY

It was a war grotesquely old fashioned in the way it consumed young lives. (Above) A Pasdaran soldier wades through mud and silt on the Howaza battlefront. He was killed later the same day.

Fue una guerra grotesca, a la antigua usanza, que se cobró muchas vidas jóvenes. (Arriba) Un soldado de Pasdaran camina entre el barro y el cieno en el campo de batalla de Howaza. Lo mataron ese mismo día.

Fu una guerra grottesca e all'antica per il modo in cui stroncò molte giovani vite. (In alto) Un pasdaran attraversa faticosamente l'acqua fangosa e il limo del campo di battaglia di Howaza. Morì lo stesso giorno, poche ore dopo.

Tragic triumph. A victorious *mullah* raises his rifle in salute as he stands above a pile of Iraqi corpses.

Trágica victoria. Un triunfante *mulá* levanta el rifle a modo de saludo, alzado sobre un montón de cadáveres de iraquíes.

Tragico trionfo. Un vittorioso mullah brandisce il suo fucile in segno di omaggio troneggiando su una pila di cadaveri iracheni.

ALFRED/LIAISON AGENCY

Hostage situations. (Left) Members of the SAS successfully raid the Iranian Embassy in London, 5 May 1980. (Opposite) US hostages arrive home after 444 days captivity in Iran, January 1981.

Liberación de rehenes. (Izquierda) Miembros del Servicio Aéreo Especial Británico logran asaltar la embajada iraní en Londres, el 5 de mayo de 1980. (Página siguiente) Rehenes estadounidenses vuelven a casa después de 444 días de cautividad en Irán, enero de 1981.

Liberazione di ostaggi. (A sinistra) Membri del SAS mentre irrompono con successo nell'ambasciata iraniana a Londra, 5 maggio 1980. (Pagina a fianco) Alcuni ostaggi americani tornano a casa dopo 444 giorni di prigionia in Iran, gennaio 1981.

PA

ANDY HERNANDEZ/COLORIFIC!

The Soviet Vietnam. Soldiers from the Red Army parade in Kabul in the early 1980s. 'The first thing which surprised me was the countryside, the Asian moon, the stars. I felt like a tourist…' – a young Russian recruit in Afghanistan.

El Vietnam soviético. Desfile de soldados del Ejército Rojo por Kabul a principios de los años ochenta. "Lo primero que me sorprendió fue el paisaje, la luna asiática, las estrellas. Me sentía como un turista…", declaró un joven recluta ruso en Afganistán.

Il Vietnam sovietico. Soldati dell'Armata Rossa sfilano a Kabul agli inizi degli anni Ottanta. "La prima cosa da cui rimasi colpito fu la campagna, la luna asiatica, le stelle. Mi sentivo come un turista…" – parole di un soldato russo in Afghanistan.

JOSEF POLLEROSS/ANZENBERGER/COLORIFIC!

Members of the *mujahedin* on guard near their base at Jagdalak, Afghanistan, February 1987. The USSR lost more than 20,000 men, the *mujahedin* more than a million. 'You wonder what the point was', wrote a Russian conscript.

Miembros del movimiento muyahidin de guardia cerca de su base en Jagdalak, Afganistán, febrero de 1987. La URSS sufrió más de 20.000 bajas; los muyahidin, más de un millón. "Te preguntabas qué sentido tenía", escribió un recluta ruso.

Alcuni *mujaheddin* di guardia vicino la loro base a Jagdalak, Afghanistan, febbraio 1987. La URSS perse più di 20.000 uomini, e i *mujaheddin* oltre un milione. "Ci si chiede quale fosse lo scopo di questa guerra", scriveva una recluta russa.

The People's Committees take to the streets of Tripoli after a TV broadcast by Colonel Gaddafi following US bombing raids on Libya, 16 April 1986.

Los comités populares toman las calles de Trípoli tras una aparición del coronel Gaddafi en televisión tras los bombardeos de Libia por parte de Estados Unidos, el 16 de abril de 1986.

I comitati popolari si riversano sulle strade di Tripoli dopo un comunicato televisivo del colonnello Gheddafi in seguito ai bombardamenti aerei degli americani sulla Libia, 16 aprile 1986.

A child's foot protrudes from the rubble of a building destroyed during the US raids on Libya, April 1986. The raids were in retaliation for the death of one US soldier killed in a terrorist attack on a West Berlin discotheque.

El pie de un niño aparece entre los escombros de un edificio destruido durante los ataques aéreos estadounidenses a Libia en abril de 1986. Los bombardeos se produjeron en represalia por la muerte de un soldado estadounidense en un atentado terrorista contra una discoteca de Berlín Oeste.

Il piede di un bambino sporge dalle macerie di un edificio distrutto durante i bombardamenti statunitensi sulla Libia, aprile 1986. Gli attacchi furono una rappresaglia contro la morte di un soldato americano rimasto ucciso in un attacco terrorista a una discoteca di Berlino Ovest.

CHRISTOPHER MORRIS/BLACK STAR/COLORIFIC!

Policing the world. One of the 26,000 US troops who entered Panama on 20 December 1989. The fighting was unexpectedly heavy and some 1,500 people were killed.

El mantenimiento del orden mundial. Uno de los 26.000 soldados estadounidenses que entraron en Panamá el 20 de diciembre de 1989. Fue una lucha de una crudeza inesperada, que se cobró 1.500 víctimas.

Mantenendo l'ordine mondiale. Uno dei 26.000 soldati americani che penetrarono a Panama il 20 dicembre del 1989. I combattimenti furono più duri del previsto e più di 1.500 persone persero la vita.

Before US intervention in Panama, President Noriega faced military revolt from within in 1988. This was backed by some of the civilian population with stones for bullets and tables for barricades.

En 1988, antes de la intervención estadounidense en Panamá, el presidente Noriega se enfrentó con una revuelta militar interna, respaldada por parte de la población civil, que luchaba con piedras en lugar de balas y utilizaba mesas a modo de barricadas.

Prima dell'intervento americano a Panama, nel 1988 il presidente Noriega aveva dovuto affrontare la rivolta militare interna. Alcuni civili vi presero parte utilizzando pietre anziché pallottole e tavoli al posto di barricate.

M. NAYTHONS/LIAISON AGENCY

The scene: a quiet road on the Caribbean island of Grenada. The time: October 1983. The sign reads 'Communism stops here'. The absurd pretext for the invasion was that the new regime on the island posed a threat to the security of the United States.

La escena: un tranquilo camino de la isla caribeña de Granada. Época: octubre de 1983. El cartel dice "El comunismo se acaba aquí". La invasión se efectuó con el absurdo pretexto de que el nuevo régimen de la isla representaba una amenaza para Estados Unidos.

La scena: una strada tranquilla sull'isola caraibica di Grenada. Il periodo: ottobre 1983. Il cartello dice: "Il comunismo finisce qui". L'assurdo pretesto che causò l'invasione fu che il nuovo regime dell'isola costituiva una minaccia per la sicurezza degli Stati Uniti.

An American soldier stands guard over a Panamanian suspect in the aftermath of the US invasion to oust Noriega, 26 December 1989.

Un soldado estadounidense vigila a un sospechoso panameño tras la invasión de Estados Unidos, que pretendía expulsar a Noriega, 26 de diciembre de 1989.

Un soldato americano sorveglia un sospetto panamense nel periodo successivo all'invasione statunitense destinata a scacciare Noriega, 26 dicembre 1989.

RAPHAEL GAILLARDE/LIAISON AGENCY

Prelude to Irangate. A US helicopter brings
supplies to the anti-government Contra rebels
in northern Nicaragua, April 1987. President
Reagan's support for the rebels brought him
into conflict with Congress, and eventually
led to the Irangate affair.

El preludio del Irangate. Un helicóptero
estadounidense suministra provisiones a
los rebeldes de la Contra en el norte de
Nicaragua, abril de 1987. El apoyo
de Reagan a los rebeldes lo enfrentó con
el Congreso estadounidense y finalmente
desembocó en el caso Irangate.

Preludio dell'Irangate. Un elicottero
americano porta provviste ai ribelli
antisandinisti dei Contras, nel nord
del Nicaragua, aprile 1987. Il sostegno
del presidente Reagan alla causa dei ribelli
gli provocò l'ostilità del Congresso, e sfociò
poi nello scandalo Irangate.

RON KINNEY/BLACK STAR/COLORIFIC!

Obeying the power that arms them. A training camp for Nicaraguan Contra
guerrillas, somewhere in Honduras, February 1989. The civil war was ebbing
to a close and towards peaceful elections one year later.

Sometidos al poder que les suministra las armas. Campo de entrenamiento
de las guerrillas de la Contra nicaragüense en Honduras, febrero de 1989.
La guerra civil llegaba a su fin. Un año más tarde se celebrarían elecciones.

Sottomissione al potere che li arma. Un campo di addestramento per i
guerriglieri dei Contras nicaraguensi, in una zona dell'Honduras, febbraio
1989. La guerra civile volgeva ormai al termine e si andava verso delle elezioni
pacifiche, svoltesi un anno più tardi.

Mocking the hand that feeds them. Athletic adolescents leap to spray revolutionary slogans on a giant McDonald's billboard in El Salvador, 15 March 1989. The presidential elections were a few days away.

Burlándose de quien los alimenta. Unos atléticos adolescentes saltan para pintar eslóganes revolucionarios con *spray* sobre una enorme valla publicitaria de McDonald's en El Salvador, 15 de marzo de 1989. Faltaban pocos días para las elecciones presidenciales.

Sputare sul piatto in cui si mangia. Due adolescenti atletici saltano per cercare di scrivere con bombolette spray degli slogan rivoluzionari su un cartellone gigante della McDonald's nello stato di El Salvador, 15 marzo 1989. Mancavano pochi giorni per le elezioni presidenziali.

CHRISTOPHER MORRIS/BLACK STAR/COLORIFIC!

Water cannon in action on the streets of Santiago, Chile, 13 September 1988.
The security forces had been called out to disperse crowds protesting at the use
of torture by the Pinochet regime.

Cañón de agua en acción en las calles de Santiago de Chile el 13 de septiembre
de 1988. Se requirió la intervención de las fuerzas de seguridad para dispersar
a la multitud que protestaba por las torturas del régimen de Pinochet.

Cannoni ad acqua in azione sulle strade di Santiago, Cile, 13 settembre 1988.
Le forze di sicurezza erano state chiamate per disperdere la folla che protestava
contro l'uso della tortura da parte del regime di Pinochet.

CHRISTOPHER MORRIS/BLACK STAR/COLORIFIC!

A month later, full-scale riots broke out in Santiago following a plebiscite in which Chileans voted for an end to the fifteen-year dictatorship of General Augusto Pinochet.

Un mes más tarde estallaron disturbios de importancia en Santiago de Chile, después del plebiscito en el que los chilenos decidieron con su voto poner fin a quince años de dictadura del general Augusto Pinochet.

Un mese dopo, scoppiarono delle vere e proprie sommosse, in seguito a un plebiscito in cui i cileni votarono per mettere fine alla dittatura, in atto da 15 anni, del generale Augusto Pinochet.

EL ESPECTADOR/SIPA PRESS

Soldiers and tanks surround the Palace of Justice, home of the Supreme
Court of Colombia, 8 November 1985. The building, in the centre of
Bogota, had been occupied by the revolutionary leftist group M-19.

Soldados y tanques rodeando el Palacio de Justicia, sede del Tribunal
Supremo de Colombia, el 8 noviembre de 1985. El edificio, situado
en el centro de Bogotá, había sido ocupado por el grupo izquierdista
revolucionario M-19.

Soldati e carri armati circondano il Palazzo di Giustizia, sede della Corte
Suprema della Colombia, 8 novembre 1985. L'edificio, nel centro di
Bogotà, era stato occupato dal gruppo rivoluzionario di sinistra M-19.

When the Palace was taken by storm more than 100 people were killed, including the President of the Supreme Court and thirty members of M-19.

En el asalto al Palacio murieron más de cien personas, entre ellos el presidente del Tribunal Supremo y treinta miembros del M-19.

Il palazzo fu preso d'assalto e più di 100 persone rimasero uccise; tra queste, il presidente della Corte Suprema e trenta membri del gruppo M-19.

COLOMBIANOS LAS ARMAS
OS HAN DADO INDEPENDENCIA
LAS LEYES OS DARÁN LIBERTAD
SANTANDER

CHRISTOPHER MORRIS/BLACK STAR/COLORIFIC!

Life and death on the streets of Medellín, Colombia, 1989: the victim of a gang who came through a bedroom window, tortured and raped her before finally killing her.

Vida y muerte en las calles de Medellín, Colombia, 1989: en la imagen, una víctima de una banda callejera. Después de entrar por la ventana de su dormitorio, los delincuentes la torturaron, violaron y finalmente la mataron.

Vita e morte sulle strade di Medellín, Colombia, 1989: la vittima di una banda che dopo aver fatto irruzione nella sua stanza da letto attraverso la finestra, l'ha torturata, stuprata e infine uccisa.

Armed civil officers of the DOC (Colombian security forces) on night patrol. The photographer described his arrival in Medellín as entering 'the gates of hell'.

Agentes civiles armados de la DOC (cuerpo de seguridad colombiano) durante una patrulla nocturna. El fotógrafo describió su llegada a Medellín como la entrada por las "puertas del infierno".

Poliziotti in borghese armati del DOC (forze di sicurezza colombiane) durante una ronda notturna. Il fotografo descrisse il suo arrivo a Medellín come l'ingresso alle "porte dell'inferno".

The Royal Navy
frigate HMS *Antelope*
is torn apart by an
Argentinian bomb,
San Carlos Bay,
Falkland Islands,
24 February 1982.

Explosión de la
fragata de la marina
real británica
Antelope como
consecuencia de una
bomba argentina,
bahía de San Carlos,
islas Malvinas,
24 de febrero
de 1982.

La fregata della
Marina reale
britannica *Antelope*
viene dilaniata da una
bomba argentina,
nella baia di San
Carlos, presso
le isole Falkland,
24 febbraio 1982.

MARTIN CLEAVER/PA

Survivors from HMS *Sir Galahad* are hauled ashore at Bluff Cove, East Falkland, 29 June 1982.
'A red alert went. We hit the deck and I saw this great orange and red streak. Trouble was, I
watched and didn't protect my face…' – Simon Weston.

Los supervivientes del buque *Sir Galahad* en su traslado a la orilla de Bluff Cove, al este de las
Malvinas, el 29 de junio de 1982. Simon Weston declaró: "Hubo una alerta roja. Caímos en
la cubierta y vi un gran rayo naranja y rojo. Me quedé mirando en vez de protegerme la cara".

Alcuni sopravvissuti della nave britannica *Sir Galahad* vengono tratti a riva a Bluff Cove, nelle
orientali Falkland, 29 giugno 1982. "Scattò l'allarme rosso. Raggiungemmo la coperta e vidi questo
gran bagliore arancione e rosso. Il problema fu che osservavo tutto senza proteggermi il volto…".
Testimonianza di Simon Weston.

TOM SMITH/EXPRESS NEWSPAPERS/HULTON|ARCHIVE

British paratroopers carry a wounded soldier to safety while under fire on Mount Longdon during the Falklands campaign, 12–13 July 1982.

Unos paracaidistas británicos trasladan a un lugar seguro a un soldado herido en una batalla en el monte Longdon durante la guerra de las Malvinas, 12–13 de julio de 1982.

Tra gli spari alcuni paracadutisti britannici portano in salvo un soldato ferito, a Mount Longdon, durante la campagna delle Falkland, 12–13 luglio 1982.

PA

The spoils of war. The fields around Goose Green are littered with
the abandoned helmets of the Argentine soldiers who surrendered
to British Falklands Task Force troops, 21 May 1982.

Botín de guerra. Los campos de alrededor de Goose Green, cubiertos
de cascos abandonados por los soldados argentinos que se rindieron
a las tropas británicas destinadas a las Malvinas, 21 de mayo de
1982.

Il bottino di guerra. I campi attorno Goose Green sono disseminati
dei caschi abbandonati dai soldati argentini, dopo la loro resa alle
truppe britanniche della Task Force delle Falkland, 21 maggio 1982.

British troops escort an Argentinian prisoner of war. He was one of the lucky ones. More than 1,000 men died serving the governments of Britain and Argentina in their squabble over a group of islands at the bottom of the world.

Soldados británicos escoltando a un prisionero de guerra argentino. Fue afortunado: más de mil soldados murieron al servicio de los gobiernos de Gran Bretaña y Argentina en su disputa por un archipiélago situado en los confines del planeta.

Le truppe britanniche scortano un prigioniero di guerra argentino; è uno dei pochi fortunati che riuscirono a sopravvivere. Oltre 1.000 uomini morirono servendo i governi della Gran Bretagna e dell'Argentina, impegnati in un assurdo alterco su un gruppo di isole in capo al mondo.

Sikhs surrender to units of the Indian army on the outskirts of the Golden Temple, Amritsar, early in 1984.

Los sijs se rinden al ejército indio en las afueras del Templo Dorado de Amritsar a principios de 1984.

Alcuni sikh si arrendono all'esercito indiano, nei pressi del Tempio d'Oro, ad Amritsar, agli inizi del 1984.

PABLO BARTHOLOMEW/LIAISON AGENCY

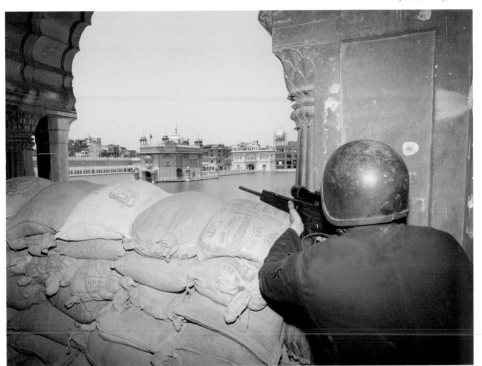

PABLO BARTHOLOMEW/LIAISON AGENCY

After the Sikh movement for greater political and religious autonomy led to clashes with Hindus, the Indian Prime Minister Indira Gandhi ordered troops into Amritsar. More than 1,000 people were killed in subsequent fighting.

Después de que el movimiento sij en favor de una mayor autonomía política y religiosa se enfrentara con los hindúes, la primera ministra india Indira Gandhi ordenó la entrada de tropas en Amritsar. En el conflicto posterior hubo más de mil víctimas mortales.

In seguito agli scontri del movimento sikh, che lottava per una maggiore autonomia politica e religiosa, con gli indù, il primo ministro indiano Indira Gandhi ordinò alle truppe di occupare Amritsar. Nei combattimenti che ne seguirono morirono più di 1.000 persone.

NICKELSBERG/LIAISON AGENCY

Intercommunal violence swept Sri Lanka in the early 1980s. President Junius Jayawardine gave wide-ranging powers to his security forces to combat Tamil separatist groups. (Above) Civilians are caught in the crossfire between rival gangs.

La violencia entre comunidades rivales arrasó Sri Lanka a principios de la década. El presidente Junius Jayawardine concedió amplios poderes a las fuerzas de seguridad para combatir los grupos separatistas tamiles. (Arriba) Civiles atrapados durante un tiroteo entre bandas rivales.

Agli inizi degli anni Ottanta lo Sri Lanka venne dilaniato da una violenza intercomunitaria. Il presidente Junius Jayawardine diede pieni poteri alle proprie forze di sicurezza per combattere i gruppi separatisti tamil. (In alto) Civili tra i fuochi di bande rivali.

NICKELSBERG/LIAISON AGENCY

Fire, looting and murder erupted on the streets of Colombo (above), and thousands of Tamils fled to the north of the island. In 1983 alone, some 380 people were killed in battles between Tamils and Singhalese.

Los incendios, los pillajes y los asesinatos invadieron las calles de Colombo (arriba), y miles de tamiles huyeron para refugiarse en el norte de la isla. Solo en 1983 murieron más de 380 personas en batallas entre tamiles y cingaleses.

Per le strade di Colombo, scontri a fuoco, atti di sciacallaggio e carneficine (in alto). Migliaia di tamil furono costretti a scappare nel nord dell'isola. Soltanto nel 1983, circa 380 persone persero la vita negli scontri tra tamil e singalesi.

Not for the first or the last time, violence breaks out in the Occupied Territories. Palestinian women and children prepare to do battle with Israeli forces.

Ni por primera ni por última vez, estalla la violencia en los territorios ocupados. Mujeres y niños palestinos se preparan para combatir al ejército israelí.

Non è la prima né l'ultima volta che la violenza scoppia nei territori occupati. Donne e bambini palestinesi si preparano per la battaglia contro le truppe israeliane.

ARAL/SIPA PRESS

A mother hurries to safety across the rubble of Beirut during an Israeli
bombardment, June 1982. The Israeli invasion of 90,000 troops, code-named
'Peace for Galilee', was intended to drive out the PLO. It failed.

Una madre corre en busca de un lugar seguro entre los escombros de Beirut
durante un bombardeo israelí, en junio de 1982. La invasión israelí, que supuso
la movilización de 90.000 soldados, fue bautizada "Paz para Galilea" y tenía la
misión de acabar con la OLP. Fracasó.

Una madre cerca di mettersi al riparo tra le macerie di Beirut durante i
bombardamenti israeliani, giugno 1982. L'obiettivo dell'invasione di 90.000
soldati israeliani, il cui nome in codice fu "Pace per la Galilea", era quello di
scacciare l'OLP. L'invasione fallì.

Ali Jawad is executed by the Amal militia in south Beirut, 30 November 1986. He had been accused of planting bombs that had killed eight people and injured forty-five others in Shiite neighbourhoods.

Ejecución de Ali Jawad a cargo de la milicia de Amal en el sur de Beirut, el 30 de noviembre de 1986. Se le había acusado de colocar en barrios chiitas unas bombas que habían matado a ocho personas y herido a otras 45.

L'esecuzione di Ali Jawad da parte delle milizie di Amal a sud di Beirut, 30 novembre 1986. Era stato accusato di aver piazzato delle bombe che avevano ucciso otto persone e ne avevano ferite altre 45 nei quartieri sciiti.

A civilian carries a baby from the wreckage of
a building in west Beirut, 1983. By this time,
anarchy reigned in what was left of the city,
with fighting between Druze militiamen,
Christians, units of the Lebanese army and
Shiite fighters.

Un civil saca a un bebé de las ruinas de un
edificio del oeste de Beirut, 1983. En aquella
época reinaba la anarquía en lo que quedaba
de la ciudad, con enfrentamientos entre
milicianos drusos, crisitianos, unidades
del ejército libanés y guerreros chiitas.

Un civile porta in salvo un bambino dallo
sfacelo di un edificio nella zona occidentale
di Beirut, 1983. All'epoca, regnava l'anarchia
in ciò che rimaneva della città, dilaniata dai
combattimenti tra le milizie druse, quelle
cristiane, le unità dell'esercito libanese e i
combattenti sciiti.

DURAND/SIPA PRESS

1985 was an unhappy year in South Africa. It was the 25th anniversary of the
Sharpeville Massacre, and violence erupted yet again. (Above) Mourners give
the African salute at a funeral in Kwa-Thena, July 1985.

1985 fue un año triste en Sudáfrica. En el vigésimoquinto aniversario de la
masacre de Sharpeville, volvió a estallar la violencia. (Arriba) Los asistentes
a un funeral en Kwa-Thena saludan a la manera africana, julio de 1985.

Il 1985 non fu un anno felice per il Sud Africa. Ricorreva il 25° anniversario del
massacro di Sharpeville, e la violenza scoppiò nuovamente. (In alto) I parenti dei
defunti fanno il saluto africano nel corso di un funerale a Kwa-Thena, luglio 1985.

Desmond Tutu, Bishop of Johannesburg and winner of the 1984 Nobel Peace Prize, speaks at the same funeral.

Desmond Tutu, obispo de Johannesburgo y ganador del premio Nobel de la Paz de 1984, interviene en el mismo funeral.

Desmond Tutu, vescovo di Johannesburg e vincitore del premio Nobel per la pace nel 1984, prende la parola durante lo stesso funerale.

DURAND/SIPA PRESS

J KUUS/SIPA PRESS

Black on white. Angry black strikers turn on their attackers after the South African police fired tear-gas canisters at a crowd in the Johannesburg suburb of Doorfontein, 22 April 1987.

Negro sobre blanco. Huelguistas negros furiosos se vuelven contra sus atacantes, después de que la policía sudafricana lanzara gas lacrimógeno en el barrio de Doorfontein, a las afueras de Johannesburgo, 22 de abril de 1987.

Neri contro bianchi. Presi dalla rabbia, alcuni scioperanti neri attaccano i loro aggressori dopo che la polizia sudafricana aveva lanciato bombolette di gas lacrimogeno contro la folla nel quartiere di Doorfontein, Johannesburg, 22 aprile 1987.

REZA/BLACK STAR/COLORIFIC!

White on black. Two members of the South African security forces lay into a young black on the street in one of the townships around Capetown. It was a time of escalating violence throughout South Africa.

Blanco sobre negro. Dos agentes de las fuerzas de seguridad sudafricanas arremeten contra un joven negro en la calle, en un distrito de los alrededores de Ciudad del Cabo. Era una época de escalada de violencia en toda Sudáfrica.

Bianchi contro neri. Due membri delle forze di sicurezza sudafricane attaccano un giovane di colore per le strade di una township vicino Capetown. In quel periodo l'escalation di violenza colpì tutto il Sudafrica.

JOHN GUNSTON/SIPA PRESS

War and deprivation. Female recruits undergo basic training to enable them to take their part in the civil war that ravaged Ethiopia during the 1980s. Women joined both Christian and Muslim armies.

Guerra y miseria. Mujeres reclutas siguen un entrenamiento básico para participar en la guerra civil que arrasó Etiopía en la década de los ochenta. Las mujeres se enrolaron en los ejércitos de los dos bandos, cristiano y musulmán.

Guerra e miseria. Addestramento di base per alcune reclute in vista della guerra civile che sconvolse l'Etiopia durante gli anni Ottanta. Le donne si arruolarono sia negli eserciti cristiani che musulmani.

OWEN/BLACK STAR/COLORIFIC!

Although much of Africa suffered drought and famine in the 1980s, it was the plight of Ethiopia which engaged the world's attention. (Above) Starving refugees wait patiently for the next distribution of food, water and medical aid, 1985.

Aunque gran parte de África sufrió sequías y hambrunas en los años ochenta, fue la difícil situación que vivió Etiopía lo que atrajo la atención mundial. (Arriba) Refugiados hambrientos esperan pacientemente el siguiente reparto de alimentos, agua y medicamentos, 1985.

Sebbene negli anni Ottanta gran parte dell'Africa fu colpita dalla siccità e dalla carestia, ad attirare l'attenzione mondiale fu la terribile situazione dell'Etiopia. (In alto) L'attesa di alcuni rifugiati affamati che aspettano con pazienza la prossima spartizione di cibo, acqua e medicine, 1985.

A Sudanese policeman attempts to hold back hundreds of starving refugees, 15 July 1985. The crowd began to surge forward the moment a small amount of relief grain arrived from the Save the Children Fund.

Un policía sudanés intenta contener a cientos de refugiados hambrientos, 15 de julio de 1985. La multitud empezó a avanzar en tropel en cuanto llegó una pequeña cantidad de alimentos, proporcionados por la fundación Save the Children.

15 luglio 1985. Un poliziotto sudanese cerca di contenere centinaia di rifugiati affamati. La folla cominciò a spingersi in avanti all'arrivo di una piccola quantità di aiuti umanitari da parte del fondo *Save the Children*.

PA

Some of the 30,000 women who formed a ring of peace round the US air force base at Greenham Common, England, on 12 December 1982. Men were excluded, and told to run the crèche and prepare the food.

Algunas de las 30.000 mujeres que formaron una cadena por la paz alrededor de la base aérea estadounidense de Greenham Common, en Inglaterra, el 12 de diciembre de 1982. Se excluyó a los hombres, a los que se les confió la cocina y el cuidado de los niños.

Alcune delle 30.000 donne che formarono un cerchio di pace attorno alla base aerea americana di Greenham Common, Inghilterra, 12 dicembre 1982. Gli uomini furono esclusi, a loro spettò il compito di occuparsi dei bambini e di preparare da mangiare.

DAVEY/DAILY EXPRESS/HULTON|ARCHIVE

Police surround striking miners as 'blackleg' drivers deliver fuel to a power station at the height of the miners' dispute, 1984. It was seen by many as a heroic if bitter last stand by organised labour in Britain and, ultimately, as a betrayal by the Government.

La policía rodea a los mineros en huelga, mientras unos camioneros esquiroles transportan carburante a una central eléctrica, en pleno conflicto minero, en 1984. Muchos consideraron la huelga como la última actuación del sindicalismo en Gran Bretaña, tan heroica como amarga, y, en el fondo, también como una traición del Gobierno.

Uno dei momenti culminanti della controversia dei minatori, 1984. La polizia circonda alcuni scioperanti mentre dei "crumiri" consegnano carburante ad una stazione elettrica. Da molti venne considerato come l'ultimo atto eroico e al contempo amaro da parte dei sindacati britannici, e sostanzialmente come un tradimento da parte del Governo.

A policeman drags a protester away from a rally by the extreme right wing National Front Party, Lewisham, south London, 21 April 1980.

Un policía aparta a un manifestante de un mitin del partido de extrema derecha Frente Nacional en Lewisham, sur de Londres, el 21 de abril de 1980.

Un poliziotto trascina via un dimostrante dalla manifestazione del partito dell'estrema destra National Front Party, a Lewisham, a sud di Londra, 21 aprile 1980.

KEYSTONE/HULTON|ARCHIVE

Meanwhile, in Toxteth… A policeman stands silhouetted against blazing buildings following race riots in the Liverpool suburb of Toxteth, July 1981. It was the first time the police had used CS gas on mainland Britain.

Mientras tanto, en Toxteth… Silueta de un policía frente a edificios ardiendo como consecuencia de los disturbios raciales en el barrio de Toxteth, a las afueras de Liverpool, en julio de 1981. Era la primera vez que la policía utilizaba gas lacrimógeno en Gran Bretaña.

Nel frattempo a Toxteth… La sagoma di un poliziotto davanti ad alcuni edifici in fiamme, dopo i disordini razziali nel sobborgo di Toxteth a Liverpool, luglio 1981. Per la prima volta in Gran Bretagna, la polizia fece uso di gas lacrimogeno.

Keeping up the bad work...
Members of the Ku Klux Klan
raise the fiery cross at Stone
Mountain, Georgia,
September 1985.

Continuando con sus felonías...
Miembros del Ku Klux Klan alzan
una cruz en llamas en Stone
Mountain, Georgia, septiembre
de 1985.

Le cattive azioni non si
arrestano... Membri del Ku Klux
Klan sollevano le croci infuocate
presso Stone Mountain,
Georgia, settembre 1985.

3. All fall down
Derrumbamientos
Tutto crolla

More fun than lessons. A pupil from a West Berlin school chips away at the Berlin Wall, 14 November 1989. Teachers organised field trips so that their classes could take home souvenir pieces of the Wall.

Más divertido que ir a clase. Un alumno de una escuela de Berlín occidental desconcha el Muro de Berlín, 14 de noviembre de 1989. Los profesores organizaron excursiones al muro para que sus alumnos se pudieran llevar a casa un trocito de recuerdo.

Più divertente delle lezioni. Un'alunna di una scuola di Berlino Ovest intacca con un martello il Muro di Berlino, 14 novembre 1989. Gli insegnanti organizzarono gite di istruzione per permettere ai loro studenti di portare a casa come souvenir pezzi del Muro.

3. All fall down
Derrumbamientos
Tutto crolla

When it came, the end was swift. For forty years or more, Eastern Europe had looked to the Soviet Union for everything – subsidies, protection, guidance, regulation, oppression, control. The monolithic structure had trembled occasionally, as in 1956 and again in 1968, but the 'evil empire' of Reagan's imagination seemed set to last forever.

In 1980 shipyard workers from Gdansk, Poland, led by Lech Walesa, forced their government to acknowledge the rights of free trade unions. Over the next ten years Walesa and the Solidarity movement nibbled away at the state's powers. There was unrest in Czechoslovakia, Romania, Hungary and East Germany. Incapable of change, Communist leaders responded by clamping down, making arrests, restricting freedom. The greatest impetus for reform came from the Soviet Union itself. In March 1985 Mikhail Gorbachev was appointed general secretary of the Communist Party. He brought a new directness, not least with his habit of turning to his advisers after a briefing and asking: 'Do you really believe what you're telling me?' The writing was on the Wall.

Cuando por fin llegó, el cambio se efectuó con rapidez. Durante más de cuarenta años, Europa del Este había vivido bajo la influencia de la Unión Soviética en todos los sentidos; de ella había recibido subsidios, protección, orientación, regulación, opresión y control. La estructura monolítica había sufrido más de una sacudida, por ejemplo en 1956 y 1968, pero el "imperio del mal" imaginado por Ronald Reagan parecía dispuesto a durar eternamente.

En 1980, los trabajadores de los astilleros de Gdansk, Polonia, liderados por Lech Walesa, obligaron a su Gobierno a reconocer los derechos de los sindicatos libres. A lo largo de los diez años siguientes, Walesa y el movimiento Solidaridad fueron menoscabando los poderes estatales. Existía malestar social en Checoslovaquia, Rumanía, Hungría y Alemania del Este. Los líderes comunistas, incapaces de cambiar realmente, respondieron tomando medidas drásticas, haciendo detenciones y restringiendo las libertades. Los mayores impulsos de reforma llegaron de la propia Unión Soviética. En marzo de 1985, Mijail Gorbachov fue nombrado secretario general del Partido Comunista. El nuevo presidente soviético introdujo una nueva forma de actuar, provista de mayor franqueza, como demuestra por ejemplo su costumbre de volverse hacia sus asesores después de las reuniones informativas para preguntarles: "¿De verdad están convencidos de lo que me están contando?". En el Muro de Berlín estaba escrito el fin del bloque soviético.

Quando giunse l'ora, la fine fu veloce. Per quarant'anni o più, l'Europa dell'Est aveva fatto affidamento sull'Unione Sovietica per ogni cosa – sovvenzioni, protezione, assistenza, regolamenti, oppressione, controllo. In alcune occasioni, come nel 1956 e poi nel 1968, la struttura monolitica aveva tremato, ma "l'impero del male", così come l'aveva definito Reagan, sembrava destinato a durare per sempre.

Nel 1980 i lavoratori dei cantieri navali di Gdansk, Danzica, in Polonia, guidati da Lech Walesa, costrinsero il governo a riconoscere il diritto d'esistenza dei sindacati liberi. Nel corso dei dieci anni che seguirono, Walesa e il movimento di Solidarnosch ridussero lentamente i poteri dello stato. Si verificarono disordini in Cecoslovacchia, Romania, Ungheria e Germania dell'Est. Incapaci di produrre cambiamenti, i leader comunisti risposero a colpi di repressione, arresti, e restrizioni della libertà. Il più forte stimolo di riforma venne dalla stessa Unione Sovietica. Nel marzo 1985 Mikhail Gorbaciov fu nominato segretario generale del Partito comunista. Tra i metodi nuovi e schietti adottati da Gorbaciov, va particolarmente sottolineata l'abitudine di rivolgersi, alla fine di una riunione, ai suoi consiglieri e chiedere: "Credete veramente in ciò che mi state dicendo?". La risposta è scritta sul Muro di Berlino.

LASKI/SIPA PRESS

Glasnost reaches out. Three years after coming to power in the Soviet
Union, Mikhail Gorbachev (centre, arm outstretched) visits Poland, July
1988. Behind him, in dark glasses, stands General Jaruzelski.

La *glásnost* tiende la mano. Tres años después de llegar al poder en la Unión
Soviética, Mijail Gorbachov (centro, con el brazo extendido) visita Polonia,
julio de 1988. Tras él, con gafas oscuras, el general Jaruzelski.

La *Glasnost* russa tende la mano. Tre anni dopo la sua elezione al potere
nell'Unione Sovietica, Mikhail Gorbaciov (al centro, con il braccio teso)
visita la Polonia, luglio 1988. Dietro di lui, con gli occhiali scuri, il generale
Jaruzelski.

TASS/LEHTIKUVA OY/COLORIFIC!

Perestroika from the shop floor up. Gorbachev converses with a worker at the Likhachev auto plant, Moscow. His leadership was regarded by many as a breath of fresh air – intelligent, efficient, reforming, all that previous leaders had not been.

La *perestroika* de arriba abajo. Gorbachov conversa con una trabajadora de la fábrica de automóviles Likhachev, situada en Moscú. Muchos consideraron su liderazgo como un soplo de aire fresco. Fue un político inteligente, eficiente y reformador: reunía todas las cualidades de las que carecían los líderes soviéticos anteriores.

La *Perestroika* dalla fabbrica in su. Gorbaciov parla con un'operaia nello stabilimento automobilistico di Likhachev, vicino Mosca. Da molti la sua leadership fu considerata una boccata d'aria fresca – intelligente, efficiente, riformatrice, tutte qualità che i leader precedenti non avevano mostrato.

Student demonstrators jubilantly wave the flag of freedom in Tiananmen Square, Beijing, China, May 1989.

Estudiantes se manifiestan y enarbolan la bandera de la libertad en la plaza Tiananmen, Pekín, China, mayo de 1989.

Protesta studentesca. Tre dimostranti in giubilo sventolano la bandiera della libertà nella piazza Tienanmen, Pechino, Cina, maggio 1989.

ERICA LANSNER/BLACK STAR/COLORIFIC!

MICHAEL COYNE/BLACK STAR/COLORIFIC!

The demonstration was a spontaneous expression of dissatisfaction with China's ageing leadership and lack of democratic reform. Students and radicals took up what amounted to permanent occupation of the square, until the tanks moved in.

La manifestación fue una expresión espontánea de insatisfacción por los avejentados líderes chinos y la falta de reformas democráticas en el país. Estudiantes y radicales se proponían ocupar la plaza de forma permanente, pero llegaron los tanques.

La protesta fu un'espressione spontanea di malcontento nei confronti degli obsolescenti dirigenti cinesi e della mancanza di riforme democratiche. Studenti e rivoluzionari intrapresero ciò che sarebbe diventata un'occupazione permanente della piazza, fino all'arrivo dei carri armati.

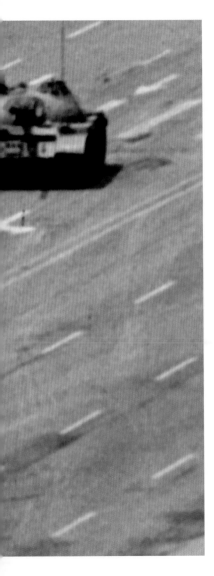

People versus power, Tiananmen Square, 5 June 1989. The man did not move; the tanks edged round him.

El pueblo contra el poder, plaza de Tiananmen, 5 de junio de 1989. El hombre no se movió; los tanques tuvieron que sortearlo.

Le persone contro il potere, piazza Tienanmen, 5 giugno 1989. L'uomo non si mosse; i carri armati gli passarono attorno.

Kiss of death.
Mikhail Gorbachev
(centre, right)
embraces East
German leader
Erich Honecker
at the end of the
German Communist
Party Conference,
East Berlin,
18 April 1986.

El beso de la muerte.
Mijail Gorbachov
(centro, derecha)
abraza al mandatario
de la República
Democrática de
Alemania Erich
Honecker tras
la clausura del
Congreso del Partido
Comunista Alemán,
Berlín Este,
18 de abril de 1986.

Il bacio della morte.
Mikhail Gorbaciov
(al centro, a destra)
abbraccia il leader
della RDT Erich
Honecker alla fine
del Congresso del
Partito socialista
tedesco (SED),
a Berlino Est,
18 aprile 1986.

East German guards
watch impassively
as Berliners batter
the Wall near the
Brandenburg
Gate, Berlin,
10 November 1989.

Policías de
la República
Democrática de
Alemania observan
impasibles cómo
los berlineses
derriban el muro
cerca de la puerta de
Brandeburgo, Berlín,
10 de noviembre de
1989.

Lo sguardo
impassibile dei
soldati della RDT
mentre i berlinesi
distruggono il Muro,
vicino alla porta
di Brandeburgo,
Berlino, 10
novembre 1989.

DAVID BRAUCHLI/REUTERS/HULTON|ARCHIVE

EPA/PA

By the following day, the Wall had been breached, leaving a gap through which tens of thousands of citizens from East Germany streamed into West Berlin. A hated symbol of division had finally been destroyed.

Al día siguiente se abrió una brecha en el Muro, por la que decenas de miles de ciudadanos de Alemania del Este entraron en tropel en Berlín Oeste. Por fin había sido destruido el tan detestado símbolo de división.

Il giorno dopo, fu aperta una breccia nel Muro che permise a decine di migliaia di cittadini della Germania dell'Est di entrare a Berlino Ovest. Finalmente, questo simbolo di divisione, così odiato, era stato distrutto.

Day trip to freedom.
A procession of
Trabant cars passes
Checkpoint Charlie
heading west,
10 November 1989.

Un día en la tierra
de la libertad.
Una procesión de
automóviles Trabant
pasa por Checkpoint
Charlie en dirección
a Berlín Oeste,
10 de noviembre
de 1989.

Una gita di un
giorno verso
la libertà. Al
Checkpoint Charlie,
una processione di
vetture Trabant si
dirigono ad ovest,
10 novembre 1989.

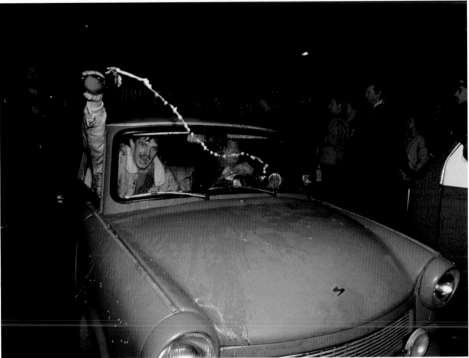

HELENE BAMBERGER/COSMOS/COLORIFIC!

They came to visit friends and relatives, to stroll along the Kurfürstendamm, to celebrate the death of a 28-year-old monster, or simply to
assure themselves that the Wall really had been breached.

Iban a visitar a amigos y parientes, a pasear por el Kurfürstendamm, a
celebrar la muerte de un monstruo que había vivido 28 largos años o
simplemente a comprobar que el Muro efectivamente había caído.

Le persone andarono a visitare parenti e amici, a passeggiare nella
Kurfürstendamm, a festeggiare la fine di un incubo durato 28 anni, o
semplicemente ad accertarsi che il Muro fosse stato veramente abbattuto.

On 9 November, the East German Government announced that 'citizens are free to travel'. Two days later the floodgates opened.

El 9 de noviembre, el Gobierno de la República Democrática de Alemania anunció que "los ciudadanos tenían libertad para viajar". Dos días después se abrieron las puertas.

Il 9 novembre, il governo della RDT annuncia che " i cittadini sono liberi di viaggiare". Due giorni dopo si aprono le cataratte.

EPA/PA

MICHAEL URBAN/REUTERS/HULTON|ARCHIVE

Joy and celebration at the Brandenburg Gate, 22 December 1989. Christmas came early to Berlin. A month earlier, the mayor of West Berlin had declared: 'The Germans are the happiest people in the world today.' The euphoria continued.

Alegría y festejos en la puerta de Brandeburgo, 22 de diciembre de 1989. La Navidad llegó a Berlín antes de tiempo. Un mes antes, el alcalde de Berlín Oeste había declarado: "El pueblo alemán es hoy el más feliz del mundo". La euforia continuaba.

Gioia e festeggiamenti davanti alla porta di Brandeburgo, 22 dicembre 1989. Il Natale arrivò in anticipo a Berlino. Un mese prima, il sindaco di Berlino Ovest aveva dichiarato: "Oggi i tedeschi sono le persone più felici al mondo". L'euforia continuava.

CHESNOT/SIPA PRESS

Before the Wall came down. Though events in Berlin attracted much attention, East Germans were on the move elsewhere. For many the route to the West was through Czechoslovakia. (Above) East German refugees enter Prague, November 1989.

Antes de la caída del Muro. Aunque los alemanes orientales estaban muy atentos a lo que sucedía en Berlín, también tenían otros destinos. Para muchos, la ruta hacia Occidente pasaba por Checoslovaquia. (Arriba) Refugiados orientales entrando en Praga, noviembre de 1989.

Prima della caduta del Muro. Sebbene gli eventi di Berlino fossero quelli più al centro dell'attenzione, i tedeschi dell'est si spostavano anche altrove. Per molti di loro la strada verso l'ovest passava dalla Cecoslovacchia. (In alto) Profughi della Germania dell'Est al loro arrivo a Praga, novembre 1989.

GUNAYDIN/SIPA PRESS

The general exodus from Eastern Europe involved others. (Above) Turkish migrant workers and their families show their passports as they near the end of their journey from Bulgaria in the summer of 1989.

El éxodo general de Europa del Este también afectó a terceros. (Arriba) Trabajadores turcos acompañados de sus familias enseñan el pasaporte al llegar al fin de su viaje desde Bulgaria, verano de 1989.

L'esodo generale dall'Europa dell'Est coinvolse altre popolazioni. (In alto) La fine del viaggio si avvicina. Alcuni emigranti turchi e le loro famiglie mentre mostrano il passaporto per poter uscire dalla Bulgaria nell'estate del 1989.

SAVESCU/SIPA PRESS

Few tried to resist the whirlwind of change that was taking place in Eastern Europe. Only in Romania was there any serious attempt to beat back the people. (Above) Crowds swarm along the streets of Bucharest, December 1989.

Pocos intentaron resistirse a los cambios vertiginosos que se producían en Europa del Este. Solamente en Rumanía se intentó seriamente reprimir al pueblo en rebelión. (Arriba) La multitud invade las calles de Bucarest, diciembre de 1989.

Pochi cercarono di resistere all'ondata di cambiamenti che si stava verificando nell'Europa dell'Est. Soltanto in Romania ci furono dei tentativi seri di reprimere la popolazione. (In alto) La folla sciama per le vie di Bucarest, dicembre 1989.

The night of change… An armed member of the Romanian security forces joins the movement for liberty, Bucharest, 22–23 December 1989.

La noche del cambio… Un miembro armado de las fuerzas de seguridad rumanas se une al movimiento por la libertad, Bucarest, 22–23 de diciembre de 1989.

La notte del cambiamento… Un membro armato delle forze di sicurezza rumene si unisce al movimento per la libertà, Bucarest, 22–23 dicembre 1989.

NICOLAS/SIPA PRESS

ANTON MANAIC/LIAISON AGENCY

(Left) Thousands gather outside the Communist Party Central Committee building in the centre of Bucharest, 22 December 1989. Feared and reviled, Ceausescu lies dead (above).

(Izquierda) Miles de personas se reúnen delante del edificio del Comité Central del Partido Comunista, en el centro de Bucarest, el 22 de diciembre 1989. (Arriba) El cadáver del temido y repudiado Ceausescu.

(A sinistra) Migliaia di persone si radunano fuori dall'edificio del Comitato centrale del Partito comunista nel centro di Bucarest, 22 dicembre 1989. Dopo essere stato temuto e insultato, Ceausescu giace ormai morto (in alto).

TOM SOBOLIK/BLACK STAR/COLORIFIC!

The return of Dubcek, Prague, November 1989. Twenty years after he had been
expelled from the Communist Party, Alexander Dubcek left the timber yard where
he had been working as a clerk, to greet crowds in the Czechoslovakian capital.

El regreso de Dubcek, Praga, noviembre de 1989. Veinte años después de ser
expulsado del Partido Comunista, Alexander Dubcek abandonó el almacén de
madera donde trabajaba como oficinista para saludar a la multitud en la capital
checoslovaca.

Il ritorno di Dubcek, a Praga, novembre 1989. Venti anni dopo essere stato espulso
dal Partito comunista, Alexander Dubcek lasciò il deposito di legname dove aveva
lavorato come impiegato, per salutare la folla riunita nella capitale cecoslovacca.

The arrival of Havel, Prague, December 1989. Ten months earlier, Václav Havel (second from left) had been imprisoned for subversion. Now he had been elected President of Czechoslovakia by popular vote.

La llegada de Havel, Praga, diciembre de 1989. Diez meses antes, Václav Havel (segundo por la izquierda) había sido encarcelado por realizar actividades subversivas. Ahora acababa de ser elegido presidente de Checoslovaquia por sufragio popular.

L'arrivo di Havel, a Praga, dicembre 1989. Dopo essere stato incarcerato per condotta sovversiva, dieci mesi dopo Václav Havel (il secondo da sinistra) viene eletto presidente della Cecoslovacchia mediante votazione popolare.

TOM SOBOLIK/BLACK STAR/COLORIFIC!

Euphoria on the streets of Prague. A delighted Czech
citizen celebrates the end of the Communist regime as
the 1980s draws to a dramatic end.

Euforia en las calles de Praga. Un alegre ciudadano
checo celebra el fin del régimen comunista: un cierre
espectacular para la década de los ochenta.

Euforia per le strade di Praga. Un cittadino ceco celebra
entusiasta la fine del regime comunista mentre gli anni
Ottanta volgono drammaticamente alla fine.

Masses on the march. Workers, students and families fill the streets of Prague during a General Strike, November 1989. The next day the Communist Prime Minister Ladislav Adamec relinquished his monopoly on power.

Manifestación masiva. Trabajadores, estudiantes y familias llenan las calles de Praga durante una huelga general en noviembre de 1989. Al día siguiente, el primer ministro Ladislav Adamec, comunista, renunció al monopolio del poder.

Dimostranti in marcia. Lavoratori, studenti e famiglie riempiono le strade di Praga durante uno sciopero generale, novembre 1989. Il giorno dopo il premier comunista Ladislav Adamec rinunciò al monopolio del potere.

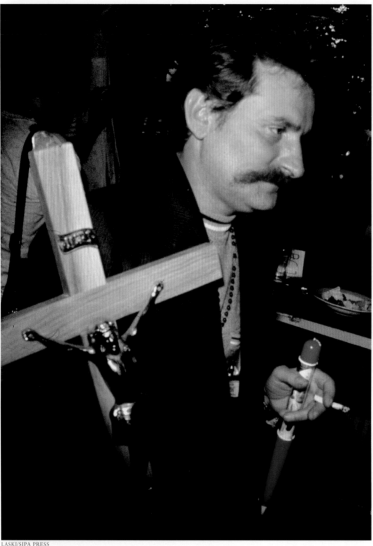

'We have achieved as much as we could…' Lech Walesa leaves the meeting at which he and the Polish Government signed an agreement establishing free trade unions, Gdansk, 1 September 1980.

"Hemos conseguido lo máximo que hemos podido…" Lech Walesa abandona la reunión en la que firmó un acuerdo con el Gobierno polaco que establecía la libertad de sindicatos, Gdansk, 1 de septiembre de 1980.

"Abbiamo ottenuto tutto ciò che siamo stati in grado di ottenere…" dichiara Lech Walesa mentre abbandona il meeting in cui lui e il governo polacco firmano un accordo che autorizza i sindacati liberi, a Gdansk, Danzica, 1 settembre 1980.

General Wojciech Jaruzelski (centre), Prime Minister of Poland and Communist Party leader, confers with army officers after placing his country under martial law, 13 December 1981.

El general Wojciech Jaruzelski (centro), primer ministro polaco y líder del Partido Comunista, conversa con oficiales del ejército tras implantar la ley marcial, 13 de diciembre de 1981.

Il generale Wojciech Jaruzelski (al centro), primo ministro polacco e leader del Partito comunista, discute con ufficiali dell'esercito dopo aver proclamato la legge marziale su tutto il paese, 13 dicembre 1981.

A smiling Lech Walesa in triumphant mood at the Gdansk Stadium, September 1983. The following month he was awarded the Nobel Peace Prize.

Lech Walesa, sonriente y victorioso, en el estadio de Gdansk, septiembre de 1983. Al mes siguiente fue galardonado con el premio Nobel de la Paz.

Un Lech Walesa sorridente e in atteggiamento trionfale allo stadio di Gdansk, Danzica, settembre 1983. Un mese dopo, gli fu concesso il premio Nobel per la pace.

4. Money
Dinero
Denaro

Worse than 1929. The *New York Post* headline describes the record slump on the American Stock Exchange as a 'Wall Street Bloodbath'. On 19 October 1987 the Dow Jones industrial average fell by 508 points.

Peor que en 1929. El titular del *New York Post* describe la caída en picado de la Bolsa estadounidense como "Baño de sangre en Wall Street". El 19 de octubre de 1987 el índice Dow Jones de Industriales descendió 508 puntos.

Peggio che nel 1929. Il *New York Post* titola "Bagno di sangue a Wall Street" per descrivere la spettacolare caduta della borsa americana. Il 19 ottobre 1987 l'indice Dow Jones segnò un calo pari a 508 punti.

4. Money
Dinero
Denaro

When the stock markets crumpled on 19 October 1987, the Crash ruined many but overall recovery was relatively quick. There was none of the drawn-out misery that followed the Wall Street Crash of 1929. Within a few months the markets had clawed their way back to pre-Crash highs.

The Eighties were years of making money in amazing amounts. At the top of the pile of gold were the entrepreneurs, the gung-ho venture capitalists. In their wake came those equally hungry for wealth but with less imagination, the willing cohorts prepared to burn themselves out for a large slice of the action. Behind them came the hopeful, content with a fast car rather than a yacht, a comfortable house rather than a palace, a case of champagne rather than the elixir of life.

The good times kept rolling. People made money hand over fist. Never had governments been more supportive; these were glory days of ever lower taxation, ever higher profits. There was nothing that money couldn't buy except perhaps anonymity.

La caída de las bolsas del 19 de octubre de 1987 arruinó a muchos inversores, pero la recuperación general llegó con relativa rapidez. Nunca llegó a producirse un interminable período de miseria similiar al que siguió al crac de Wall Street en 1929 y en pocos meses los mercados alcanzaron los altos valores anteriores a la crisis.

En la década de los ochenta se ganaron espectaculares sumas de dinero. Encabezaban la lista de las mayores fortunas los empresarios, los capitalistas más agresivos y entusiastas. Tras ellos llegaron otros igualmente ávidos de riqueza pero con menos imaginación, segundones dispuestos a todo por llevarse un pedazo del pastel. Y finalmente estaban quienes, con tanta ambición como modestia, se conformaban con un automóvil veloz en lugar de un yate, con una casa confortable en lugar de un palacio y con unas botellas de champán en lugar del elixir de la vida.

Y los buenos tiempos siguieron. Se ganó dinero a manos llenas. Los gobiernos jamás habían concedido tantas ayudas; fueron días de gloria con impuestos más bajos que nunca y beneficios que no dejaban de aumentar. No había nada que no pudiera comprar el dinero, salvo quizá el anonimato.

Il crollo delle borse del 19 ottobre 1987 fu un evento rovinoso per molti, ma la ripresa fu relativamente veloce per tutta l'economia. Non si verificò la stessa depressione costante seguita al crollo di Wall Street nel 1929. Nel giro di pochi mesi, i mercati recuperarono raggiungendo nuovamente i livelli massimi registrati prima della fatidica data.

Gli anni Ottanta furono un periodo in cui si ebbe l'opportunità di guadagnare delle ingenti somme di denaro. In cima alla lista dei più ricchi vi erano gli imprenditori, i fanatici capitalisti di ventura. Dietro le loro orme, arrivarono uomini anch'essi avidi di ricchezza ma dotati di meno immaginazione, seguiti da coorti di individui disposti a tutto pur di conquistarsi un posto al sole. Dietro di loro, vi erano gli ambiziosi più modesti che si accontentavano di un'auto veloce anziché di uno yacht, di una casa accogliente anziché di un palazzo, di una cassa di champagne anziché dell'elisir di lunga vita.

Il periodo di prosperità continuò. Le persone fecero soldi in abbondanza. I governi non erano mai stati così disposti ad ascoltare; furono questi dei giorni di gloria in cui si pagavano sempre meno tasse nonostante i guadagni fossero sempre più elevati. Non vi era niente che il denaro non potesse comprare tranne forse l'anonimato.

Alternative takes on the Market Crash. (Left) On the same day, a trader slumps in his seat on the floor of the New York Stock Exchange.

Visiones distintas del crac bursátil. (Izquierda) El mismo día de la caída, un agente de bolsa se derrumba en su silla, en el parqué de la Bolsa de Nueva York.

Reazioni differenti segnano il crollo della Borsa. (A sinistra) Lo stesso giorno, un operatore sprofonda sulla sua sedia nella Borsa di New York.

JOSEPH RODRIGUEZ/BLACK STAR/COLORIFIC!

Two days after the Crash, Freddy (a representative of the less affluent) parades outside the NY Stock Exchange. His poster sez: 'Lost money on Wall Street? Who me? I'm broke already!'

Dos días después de la caída de la Bolsa, Freddy (representante de los desposeídos) desfila por delante de la Bolsa neoyorquina. Su cartel dice: "¿Perder dinero en Wall Street? ¿Yo? ¡Pero si no tengo un céntimo!".

Due giorni dopo il crollo, Freddy (rappresentante i meno benestanti) sfila fuori la Borsa di New York. Il suo poster recita: "Hai perso soldi a Wall Street? Chi io? Io sono già rovinato!".

But the show goes on. Dealers crane forward to make their bids at the London Metal Exchange as the markets rise again in 1989.

Pero el espectáculo continúa. Corredores de bolsa dispuestos a presentar sus ofertas en la Bolsa de Londres con la nueva subida de los mercados de 1989.

Ma lo spettacolo prosegue. Gli operatori di borsa allungano il collo per fare le loro offerte alla Borsa Metalli di Londra, mentre i mercati si risollevano nel 1989.

In the wake of Wall Street. A dealer hurries to the London Stock Exchange. Black Monday (19 October) was a bad day across the Western world.

En la estela de Wall Street. Un corredor de bolsa se dirige a toda prisa a la Bolsa de Londres. El viernes negro (19 de octubre) fue un mal día en todo el mundo occidental.

Sulla scia di Wall Street. Un operatore si affretta a raggiungere la Borsa di Londra. Il lunedì nero (19 ottobre) fu un brutto giorno per tutti i mercati del mondo occidentale.

DAVID GIBSON

MALANKA/SIPA PRESS

French dealers rush to the Paris Bourse, 21 October 1987. On that day the Dow rose by a record 186 points, to recover almost half its original loss, but there were more falls to come.

Agentes de bolsa franceses corriendo hacia el edificio de la Bolsa de París el 21 de octubre de 1987. Aquel día el Dow Jones alcanzó un récord de 186 puntos, con lo que recuperó casi la mitad del valor anterior a las pérdidas. Pero habría más caídas.

Gli operatori francesi si precipitano alla Borsa di Parigi, 21 ottobre 1987. Quel giorno l'indice Dow Jones fece registrare un record, guadagnando 186 punti, e recuperando così più della metà della perdita iniziale, ma altre cadute si sarebbero verificate.

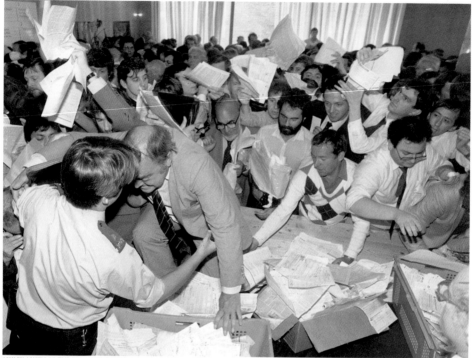

ASHLEY ASHWOOD/THE FINANCIAL TIMES

Summer greed. In August 1984 the British motor company Jaguar was floated on the Stock Exchange. (Above) Those who left their application for shares until the last day fight to hand in their forms.

Codicia estival. En agosto de 1984 salió a Bolsa la empresa automovilística británica Jaguar. (Arriba) En la imagen, las personas que esperaron hasta el último día para comprar acciones peleándose por entregar los impresos.

Avidità estiva. Nell'agosto del 1984 l'azienda automobilistica britannica Jaguar fu lanciata in borsa. (In alto) Lotta all'ultimo minuto per consegnare in tempo i moduli di sottoscrizione delle azioni.

Autumn greed.
Would-be share-
holders in the
Laura Ashley fashion
empire form a last
minute queue,
Farringdon Street,
London,
28 November 1985.

Codicia otoñal.
Los interesados en
adquirir acciones del
imperio de la moda
Laura Ashley forman
cola en las horas
previas a la
finalización del
plazo establecido,
Farringdon Street,
Londres, 28 de
noviembre de 1985.

Avidità autunnale.
Potenziali azionisti
dell'impero della
moda Laura Ashley
in fila prima della
scadenza per le
sottoscrizioni,
a Farringdon
Street, Londra,
28 novembre 1985.

PA

MARK RICHARDS/COLORIFIC!

Lending a Presidential hand – let's hope he washed them first.
President George Bush visits former industrial workers who have
retrained to work in a branch of Domino's Pizza.

El Presidente echa una mano: esperemos que se la hubiera lavado
antes. El presidente de Estados Unidos George Bush visita un
restaurante de la cadena Domino's Pizza, donde fueron recolocados
antiguos trabajadores de una fábrica.

Il presidente dà una mano – speriamo che se le sia lavate prima.
George Bush visita un ristorante di Domino's Pizza, che ha permesso
ad alcuni ex lavoratori industriali di ritrovare un impiego.

IAN TYAS/KEYSTONE/HULTON|ARCHIVE

Bending a Prime Ministerial ear. Margaret Thatcher (left) visits the Pattersons at their newly acquired home in Harold Hill, Essex. They were the 12,000th family to buy their home from the GLC (courtesy of State sell-offs).

Primera Ministra a la escucha. Margaret Thatcher (izquierda) visita a la familia Patterson en su nueva casa de Harold Hill, Essex. Fueron la familia número 12.000 en comprar su hogar al Greater London Council (cortesía del Estado).

Il Premier all'ascolto. Margaret Thatcher visita i Patterson nella loro nuova casa di Harold Hill, Essex. Sono stati la famiglia nº 12.000 ad acquistare la loro casa mediante gli aiuti dell'ente municipale Great London Council (per gentile concessione di cessioni statali).

The new tycoons. (Left) Bill Gates, founder of the Microsoft Corporation, 1985. He was well on his way to becoming the richest man in the world.

Los nuevos magnates. (Izquierda) Bill Gates, fundador de Microsoft Corporation, 1985. Poco le faltaba para ser el hombre más rico del mundo.

I nuovi magnati (a sinistra). Bill Gates, fondatore della Microsoft Corporation, 1985. Non ci avrebbe messo molto a diventare l'uomo più ricco del mondo.

(Right) Steve Jobs, co-founder of Apple Computers, and later head of Pixar Studios, makers of *Toy Story*.

(Derecha) Steve Jobs, cofundador de Apple Computers y posteriormente director de Pixar Studios, los creadores de *Toy Story*.

(A destra) Steve Jobs, cofondatore della Apple Computers e futuro direttore dei Pixar Studios, creatori di *Toy Story*.

BERNARD GOTFRYD/COLORIFIC!

TERENCE SPENCER/COLORIFIC!

Happy landings. Richard Branson plays in the bath, promoting Virgin
Atlantic Airways. The company was founded in 1984 after Branson had
been forced to sell his record empire.

Un feliz aterrizaje. Richard Branson juega en la bañera en la promoción
de Virgin Atlantic Airways. La empresa se fundó en 1984, después de
que Branson se viera obligado a vender su imperio discográfico.

Atterraggio felice. Richard Branson gioca nella vasca da bagno, facendo
pubblicità alla Virgin Atlantic Airways. La compagnia aerea fu fondata
nel 1984 dopo che Branson era stato costretto a vendere il suo impero
discografico.

Hullo, John, got a new motor...? John DeLorean proudly displays a picture of his gull-winged, stainless steel sports car. Despite massive publicity and enormous subsidies from the British Government, the car was a commercial failure.

Hola, John, ¿un motor nuevo...? John DeLorean muestra con orgullo una fotografía de su coche deportivo de acero inoxidable con puertas de apertura superior. Pese a la publicidad masiva y las cuantiosas subvenciones del Gobierno británico, el automóvil fue un fracaso comercial.

"Hullo, John got a new motor...?" John DeLorean mostra con orgoglio una foto della sua macchina sportiva in acciaio inossidabile, con porte ad ali di gabbiano. Nonostante l'imponente campagna pubblicitaria e le ingenti sovvenzioni del governo britannico, l'auto fu un fiasco commerciale.

MARIO RUIZ/COLORIFIC!

Playing the Trump card... Donald and Ivana Trump pose in the Ruby
Room of their luxury yacht the *Trump Princess*, 7 April 1988. Three
months later he acquired the *Nabila*, the largest yacht in the world.

Jugando la carta Trump... Donald e Ivana Trump posan en el salón Rubí
de su yate de lujo *Trump Princess*, 7 de abril de 1988. Tres meses después
Donald Trump adquirió el yate *Nabila*, el más grande del mundo.

La carta vincente dei Trump... Donald e Ivana Trump posano nella
Ruby Room del loro lussuoso yacht, il *Trump Princess*, 7 aprile 1988.
Tre mesi più tardi, Donald acquistò il *Nabila*, lo yacht più grande del
mondo.

Big hair day... Peter Stringfellow, owner of the eponymous London club at ease with champagne and underdressed blondes. His consumption of both was conspicious in the Eighties.

La buena vida... Peter Stringfellow, propietario del club de *striptease* londinense que lleva su nombre, bebiendo champán junto a unas cuantas rubias ligeras de ropa. Su gusto por ambos se hizo evidente en los años ochenta.

La bella vita... Peter Stringfellow, proprietario dell'omonimo club londinese, a suo agio tra una coppa di champagne e belle bionde strette in vestiti succinti. Negli anni Ottanta fu al centro dell'attenzione per il suo appariscente consumo di entrambi.

LAURENCE CENDROWICZ/COLORIFIC!

'Only the little people pay taxes…' Leona Helmsley displays hubris as she poses beside a portrait of her husband, June 1989. Her hotel empire ran into difficulties when she was accused of tax evasion on a grand scale.

"Solo los peleles pagan impuestos…" Leona Helmsley posa con un orgullo desmesurado junto a un retrato de su esposo, junio de 1989. Su imperio hotelero empezó a tener problemas cuando fue acusada de evasión de impuestos a gran escala.

"Solo gli gnomi e le fate pagano le tasse…" Leona Helmsley posa in atteggiamento borioso davanti a un ritratto del marito, giugno 1989. Il suo impero alberghiero andò incontro a delle difficoltà quando venne accusata di evasione fiscale a grande scala.

TOM IVES/BLACK STAR/COLORIFIC!

Wrapped up against the cold. A woman attempts to keep herself warm in a bus
shelter at Phoenix, Arizona, December 1983. The general increase in wealth was
accompanied by a huge rise in the number of people living in poverty.

Abrigada para protegerse del frío. Una mujer intenta entrar en calor en una parada
de autobús de Phoenix, Arizona, diciembre de 1983. El aumento general de la
riqueza fue acompañado de un enorme incremento del número de pobres.

Imbacuccata contro il freddo. Una donna cerca di riscaldarsi sotto la pensilina di un
autobus a Phoenix, Arizona, dicembre 1983. L'aumento generale delle ricchezze fu
accompagnato dall'incremento del numero di persone che vivevano in povertà.

ROGER CHARITY/COLORIFIC!

Cushioned against discomfort. Joan Collins relaxes on a sofa newly delivered from Heal's, the London furniture store. This one looked better without the plastic wrapping.

Protegida contra toda incomodidad. Joan Collins se relaja en un sofá recién entregado por la tienda de muebles londinense Heal's. Lucía más sin el plástico.

Protetta contro le scomodità. Joan Collins si rilassa su un divano appena consegnato da Heal's, il celebre negozio londinese di mobili. Il divano apparirà più chic senza l'involucro di plastica.

5. Entertainment
Espectáculos
Spettacolo

Lauren Hutton and Richard Gere make an unsuccessful attempt to avoid the attention of the press at the preview of their 1980 film *American Gigolo*, directed by Paul Schrader. Christopher Reeve had previously rejected Gere's role.

Lauren Hutton y Richard Gere intentan en vano evitar la atención de la prensa en el preestreno de su película *American Gigolo* (1980), dirigida por Paul Schrader. Christopher Reeve había rechazado el papel de Gere.

Lauren Hutton e Richard Gere tentano senza successo di evitare l'attenzione della stampa all'anteprima del loro film *American Gigolo*, del 1980, diretto da Paul Schrader. In precedenza Christopher Reeve aveva rifiutato il ruolo di Gere.

5. Entertainment
Espectáculos
Spettacolo

Times were good for the stars. Television audiences reached an all-time peak for the on-going dramas of the TV soaps *Dallas* and *Dynasty*. Film budgets reached their highest levels of all time – *Batman* cost $50 million, *Who Framed Roger Rabbit?* held the record for a while at $70 million. The returns on such massive capital outlays made it all worthwhile – *ET* alone grossed $228 million.

Much of the credit for this renewed vigour and profitability went to Steven Spielberg. Almost single-handedly he revived the notion of family outings to the cinema, with films that brought back memories of the golden days of the 1940s and early 1950s. It was a considerable achievement, for video recorders were to be found in more and more homes and the age of the couch potato was looming.

The Eighties also saw a continuation in the rise of violence on TV and cinema screen. Arnie Schwarzenegger splattered his enemies against innumerable walls; in *Die Hard* Bruce Willis did more damage to LA than the earthquake of October 1987. George Lucas completed his *Star Wars* trilogy, and science fiction became the most popular movie genre.

Eran buenos tiempos para las estrellas del espectáculo. La audencia televisiva alcanzó un máximo histórico con las series dramáticas *Dallas* y *Dinastía*. Los presupuestos cinematográficos también batieron récords: *Batman* costó 50 millones de dólares y *¿Quién engañó a Roger Rabbit?* fue en su momento la película más cara de la historia, con un coste de 70 millones de dólares. Las inmensas inversiones de capital merecieron la pena, vistos los beneficios: *E. T.* recaudó por sí sola 228 millones de dólares.

Buena parte del mérito de la revitalización y la nueva rentabilidad del cine se debió a Steven Spielberg. El director resucitó casi en solitario las salidas familiares al cine, con películas que evocaban la época dorada de los años cuarenta y principios de los cincuenta. El suyo fue todo un logro, en una época en que el vídeo entraba en un número de hogares cada vez mayor y se avecinaba la gran era del consumo pasivo de la televisión.

La escalada de violencia en la televisión y las pantallas de cine también prosiguió en los años ochenta. En sus películas, Arnold Schwarzenegger aplastaba contra los muros a incontables enemigos y en *La jungla de cristal* Bruce Willis causó más desperfectos en Los Ángeles que el terremoto de octubre de 1987. George Lucas finalizó la trilogía *La guerra de las galaxias* y la ciencia ficción se convirtió en el género cinematográfico más popular.

Fu un buon periodo per le stelle dello spettacolo. L'audience televisiva raggiunse il massimo storico con sceneggiati a puntate ricchi di vicende drammatiche, quali *Dallas* e *Dynasty*. Anche i budget dei film erano più alti che mai – *Batman* costò 50 milioni di dollari, *Chi ha incastrato Roger Rabbit?* detenne il record per un po' con 70 milioni di dollari. Visti i profitti ricavati da tali ingenti investimenti di capitale, valeva la pena rischiare – *E.T.* da solo incassò 228 milioni di dollari.

Gran parte del merito per questa rinnovata forza e redditività andò a Steven Spielberg. Fu lui che quasi da solo ravvivò il piacere delle uscite in famiglia per andare al cinema, realizzando dei film che ricordavano i tempi d'oro degli anni Quaranta e dei primi anni Cinquanta. Fu una conquista notevole, che avrebbe fatto aumentare da lì a poco il numero di famiglie in possesso di un videoregistratore; si avvicinava l'era dei teledipendenti.

Gli anni Ottanta furono testimoni inoltre di un continuo aumento della violenza sugli schermi televisivi e cinematografici. Arnold Schwarzenegger si divertiva a spiacciare nemici contro i muri; in *Trappola di cristallo* Bruce Willis causava più danni a Los Angeles che il terremoto dell'ottobre del 1987. George Lucas completava la trilogia di *Guerre Stellari*, e la fantascienza diventava il genere cinematografico più popolare.

Dan Aykroyd (left) and John Belushi hit the road after the success of John Landis's 1980 cult movie *The Blues Brothers*.

Dan Aykroyd (izquierda) y John Belushi se ponen en marcha tras el éxito de la película de culto de John Landis *Granujas a todo ritmo* (1980).

Dan Aykroyd (a sinistra) e John Belushi partono per la grande avventura dopo il successo del cult movie *The Blues Brothers*, diretto da John Landis nel 1980.

Danny de Vito and
Rhea Perlman (Carla
from *Cheers*) present
themselves as that
rare phenomenon, a
happy Hollywood
couple, 1983.

Danny de Vito y
Rhea Perlman (Carla
en la serie *Cheers*)
protagonizaron un
fenómeno inédito:
una pareja feliz en
Hollywood, 1983.

Danny de Vito e
Rhea Perlman (Carla
della serie *Cheers*)
si presentano come
una coppia felice,
un fenomeno
alquanto strano per
Hollywood, 1983.

MARK SENNET/SHOOTING STAR/COLORIFIC!

BRIAN HAMILL/HULTON|ARCHIVE

Martin Scorsese and Rosanna Arquette on the set of *New York Stories*, 1989. The film was a 'three-course meal' – three tales directed by three directors, Scorsese, Francis Ford Coppola and Woody Allen. It failed.

Martin Scorsese y Rosanna Arquette durante el rodaje de *Historias de Nueva York* (1989). La película ofrecía un "menú de tres platos", tres historias dirigidas por tres directores distintos: Scorsese, Francis Ford Coppola y Woody Allen. El proyecto fue un fracaso.

Martin Scorsese e Rosanna Arquette sul set di *New York Stories*, 1989. Il film era stato concepito come un pranzo "a tre portate", tre episodi diretti da tre registi diversi: Scorsese, Francis Ford Coppola e Woody Allen. Non ebbe successo.

JEFFREY AARONSON/COLORIFIC!

Before it fell apart… Jack Nicholson and Anjelica Huston gaze fondly at each other in Gordon's Rest, Aspen, Colorado. In the 1980s Aspen was home to many movie stars, including Nicholson, Goldie Hawn and Cher.

Antes de la ruptura… Jack Nicholson y Anjelica Huston se miran con cariño en Gordon's Rest, Aspen, Colorado. En los años ochenta, Aspen acogió a muchas estrellas del cine, entre ellos, Nicholson, Goldie Hawn y Cher.

Prima della rottura… Jack Nicholson e Anjelica Huston si guardano amorevolmente a Gordon's Rest, Aspen, Colorado. Negli anni Ottanta Aspen era il luogo dove risiedevano molte star del cinema come Nicholson, Goldie Hawn e Cher.

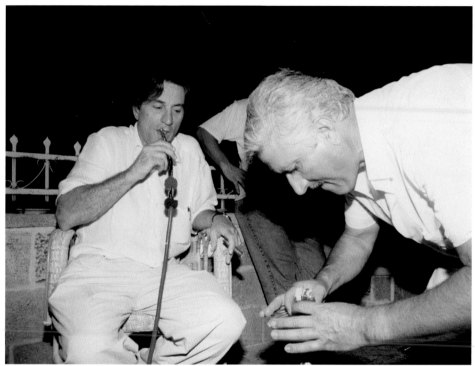

MOSHE SHAI/SHOOTING STAR/COLORIFIC!

Chilling out in the Middle East. After a hectic film schedule in the late 1970s (*Taxi Driver*, *Raging Bull* and *New York, New York*) Robert de Niro takes time off to smoke a little hash through a bong.

Un momento de descanso en Oriente Próximo. Tras una época de mucha actividad a finales de los años setenta (*Taxi Driver*, *Toro salvaje* y *New York, New York*), Robert de Niro se relaja fumando un poco de hachís en cachimba.

Un po' di relax in Medio Oriente. Dopo un programma molto intenso di riprese verso la fine degli anni Settanta (*Taxi Driver*, *Toro scatenato* e *New York, New York*) Robert de Niro si prende del tempo libero e fuma un po' di hascisc con un narghilè.

Alan Alda (left) enjoys Warren Beatty's moment of glory as the latter holds his Director's Guild of America Award for *Reds*, 13 March 1982.

Alan Alda (izquierda) disfruta junto a Warren Beatty del momento de gloria de este último, que acababa de recibir el premio del Director's Guild of America por *Rojos*, 13 de marzo de 1982.

Alan Alda (a sinistra) condivide il momento di gloria di Warren Beatty, che ha appena ricevuto il premio del Director's Guild of America al miglior regista per il film *Reds*, 13 marzo 1982.

BOB SCOTT/FOTOS INTERNATIONAL/HULTON|ARCHIVE

The price of fame. Sean Penn (left) and an almost obscured Madonna run the gauntlet of Hollywood photographers, 1985. It was the year of Madonna's first film, *Desperately Seeking Susan*.

El precio de la fama. Sean Penn (izquierda) y Madonna, prácticamente oculta, soportan el acoso de los fotógrafos de Hollywood, 1985. Fue el año del primer largometraje de Madonna, *Buscando a Susan desesperadamente*.

Il prezzo della fama. Sean Penn (a sinistra) e una Madonna quasi invisibile cercano di evitare i flash dei paparazzi hollywoodiani. Era il 1985, l'anno del primo film di Madonna, *Cercasi Susan disperatamente*.

COLORIFIC!

An actor comes face to face with reality. Nastassja Kinski gets some tips from a real bear on the set of *The Hotel New Hampshire*, 1984. Kinski played the part of Susie the bear in the movie.

Actriz cara a cara con la naturaleza. Nastassja Kinski recibe unos consejos de un oso auténtico durante el rodaje de *Hotel New Hampshire*, 1984. Kinski interpretaba a Susie, *la osa*.

Un'attrice faccia a faccia con la realtà. Nastassja Kinski riceve alcuni consigli pratici da un orso vero sul set di *Hotel New Hampshire*, 1984. Nel film, la Kinski recitò la parte di Susie l'orsa.

MAURO CARRARO/COLORIFIC!

Christopher Lambert sits with his on-screen adoptive mother on the set of Hugh Hudson's 1984 movie *Greystoke: The Legend of Tarzan, Lord of the Apes*. Some critics unkindly suggested that the apes came closer to Oscar-winning performances.

Christopher Lambert junto a su madre adoptiva en la pantalla, durante el rodaje de la película de Hugh Hudson *Greystoke, la leyenda de Tarzán, el rey de los monos* (1984). Algunos críticos señalaron con malicia que los monos merecían mucho más un *oscar* que el actor.

Christopher Lambert siede accanto alla madre adottiva sul set del film *Greystoke - La leggenda di Tarzan signore delle scimmie* diretto da Hugh Hudson nel 1984. Alcuni critici suggerirono scortesemente che più di ogni altro attore, le scimmie avrebbero meritato un Oscar alla migliore interpretazione.

CAVALIER/SHOOTING STAR/COLORIFIC!

David Hasselhoff poses beside the star of the show, a talking car, in the TV series *Knight Rider*. For Hasselhoff, ahead lay *Baywatch* and even greater fame. For the car, it was the scrap heap. That's showbiz!

David Hasselhoff posa junto a la estrella de la serie de televisión *El coche fantástico*, un coche que hablaba. A Hasselhoff el futuro le depararía *Los vigilantes de la playa* y una fama aún mayor. Al coche le esperaba el desguace: así es el mundo del espectáculo.

David Hasselhoff posa accanto alla star della situazione, una macchina parlante, nel telefilm per la TV *Supercar*. Hasselhoff sarebbe diventato ancora più famoso con la serie *Baywatch*. Mentre per la macchina non rimaneva altro che la rottamazione. Ecco come va lo *showbiz!*

Tom Selleck and his moustache try to steal the thunder from their co-star, the red Ferrari, in the TV series *Magnum*.

Tom Selleck y su bigote intentan quitarle protagonismo a su compañero de reparto en la serie televisiva *Magnum*: el Ferrari rojo.

Tom Selleck e i suoi baffi cercano di rubare protagonismo all'altra star della serie televisiva *Magnum P.I.*, una Ferrari testa rossa.

Woody Allen makes his weekly visit to Michael's Pub, Manhattan, to wail with the New Orleans Funeral and Ragtime Orchestra, 1980.

Woody Allen hace su visita semanal a Michael's Pub, en Manhattan, para tocar con la New Orleans Funeral and Ragtime Orchestra, 1980.

Woody Allen in una delle sue appassionate esibizioni settimanali al Michael's Pub, a Manhattan, con la New Orleans Funeral and Ragtime Orchestra, 1980.

Eddie Murphy takes time out from *Trading Places* wearing a white suit to do his famous impression of the young Alec Guinness at Bentley's Disco.

Eddie Murphy deja por un momento el rodaje de *Entre pillos anda el juego* y se viste con un traje blanco para interpretar su "célebre" imitación de un joven Alec Guinness transportado a la discoteca Bentley's.

Momento di relax per Eddie Murphy dopo *Una poltrona per due*. Eccolo in abito bianco mentre imita il giovane Alec Guinness alla Bentley's Disco.

LEROY WOODSON JR/COLORIFIC!

Giving the game away… How *did* they make Henry Thomas fly for *ET: The Extra Terrestrial*, Hollywood, 1982? The technique was called Blue Screen.

Desvelando el truco… ¿Cómo se consiguió que Henry Thomas volara en *E. T. el extraterrestre*, (Hollywood, 1982)? Con la técnica llamada "Blue Screen".

Ecco svelato il trucco… Come riuscirono a far volare Henry Thomas in *E.T. - L'Extraterrestre*, a Hollywood nel 1982? La tecnica si chiamava "Blue Screen".

JIM McHUGH/VISAGES/COLORIFIC!

ET's creator Steven Spielberg lines up another shot for his 1980 blockbuster *Indiana Jones and the Temple of Doom*. It was a highly profitable time for the *Wunderkind*. Just as well: his divorce cost him $100 million.

El creador de *E. T.* Steven Spielberg, encuadra un plano de *Indiana Jones y el templo maldito,* un éxito de taquilla en 1980. Fue una época muy rentable para este niño prodigio del cine. Lo necesitaría: divorciarse le costó 100 millones de dólares.

Steven Spielberg, il creatore di *E.T.,* prepara un'altra ripresa del suo film *Indiana Jones e il tempio maledetto*, un autentico successo al botteghino nel 1980. Fu un ottimo periodo con ingenti guadagni per il bambino prodigio del cinema. Meno male che il suo divorzio gli costò "solo" 100 milioni di dollari.

After a string of films for TV in the early 1980s, the British director Mike Leigh made his cinema debut in 1988 with *High Hopes*.

Después de realizar varias películas para televisión a principios de los años ochenta, el director británico Mike Leigh debutó en el cine en 1988 con *Grandes ambiciones*.

Dopo un serie di film per la TV agli inizi degli anni Ottanta, il registra britannico Mike Leigh debutta nel cinema nel 1988 con *Belle speranze*.

JOE McNALLY/COLORIFIC!

Milos Forman relaxes at home in Danbury, Connecticut, November 1984. It was the year in which his film version of Peter Shaffer's play *Amadeus* won Oscars for Best Film, Best Director (himself) and Best Actor (F. Murray Abraham).

Milos Forman descansa en su casa de Danbury, Connecticut, en noviembre de 1984. Aquel año consiguió varios *oscars* con su versión para la gran pantalla de la obra teatral de Peter Shaffer *Amadeus*: mejor película, mejor director (él) y mejor actor (F. Murray Abraham).

Milos Forman si rilassa nella sua casa di Danbury, Connecticut, novembre 1984. Fu l'anno in cui la sua versione cinematografica dell'opera di Peter Shaffer *Amadeus* vinse gli Oscar al miglior film, miglior regista (lo stesso Forman) e miglior attore (F. Murray Abraham).

The paper headline says 'How to make your wimp more macho'. The mug says 'Good @*!#@* morning'. Roseanne Barr just smiles.

El titular del periódico dice: "Cómo transformar al calzonazos de tu marido en un macho". La taza dice "Buenos @*!#@* días". Roseanne Barr simplemente sonríe.

Il titolo del giornale recita "Come trasformare il tuo fifone in un tipo più macho". La tazza dice "Good @*!#@* morning". Roseanne Barr sorride e basta.

N SHALLIT/COLORIFIC!

Student Brooke Shields takes part in a stage production at Princeton University in the mid-1980s. She already had a considerable movie career behind her, having made her debut as a child.

La alumna de Princeton Brooke Shields participa en una obra de la universidad a mediados de los años ochenta. Ya tenía a sus espaldas una notable carrera en el cine, donde debutó de niña.

Ancora studente, Brooke Shields partecipa a una produzione teatrale organizzata dalla Princeton University a metà degli anni Ottanta. Avendo debuttato quando era una bambina, Shields aveva già alle spalle una notevole carriera cinematografica.

No gain (and possibly no career) without pain. Sylvester Stallone and son work out on the lawn of their Hollywood home, 1981. Ahead lay more *Rocky* films and the bullet-riddled *First Blood*.

Para presumir (y probablemente también para hacer carrera) hay que sufrir. Sylvester Stallone y su hijo hacen ejercicio en el jardín de su casa de Hollywood en 1981. Aún rodaría más entregas de la saga *Rocky* y las diversas partes de *Rambo*.

Nessun guadagno (e forse nessuna carriera) senza un po' di sofferenza. Sylvester Stallone e il figlio si allenano sul prato della loro casa a Hollywood, 1981. Per lui il programma prevedeva altri episodi di *Rocky* e il violento *Rambo*.

COLORIFIC!

Under the bashful eye of her fitness expert, Joan Collins goes through her regime at her private gym. These were the glory years of the TV series *Dynasty*, which gained audiences world-wide.

Observada por su discreto profesor, Joan Collins realiza su programa personal de ejercicios en su gimnasio privado. Fue la época dorada de la serie televisiva *Dinastía*, que sedujo al público de todo el mundo.

Sotto lo sguardo schivo del suo professore di fitness, Joan Collins si tiene in forma esercitandosi nella sua palestra privata. Erano anni d'oro per la serie TV *Dynasty*, che ottenne elevatissimi indici di audience a livello mondiale.

YORAM KAHANA/SHOOTING STAR/COLORIFIC!

British actor Roger Moore relaxes in the comfort of a luxury limo. In the 1980s Moore gave up his Beretta, his exploding fountain pen, his catapulting wristwatch, and handed over the role of 007 to Timothy Dalton.

El actor británico Roger Moore disfruta de las comodidades de una lujosa limusina. En los años ochenta Moore abandonó su Beretta, su pluma estilográfica explosiva y su reloj de pulsera catapulta, y le cedió el papel de agente 007 a Timothy Dalton.

Momento di relax per l'attore britannico Roger Moore, dentro una comoda e lussuosa limousine. Negli anni Ottanta il ruolo di agente 007 fu affidato a Timothy Dalton; Moore dovette quindi abbandonare la sua Beretta, la penna esplosiva e l'orologio da polso catapultante.

Dudley Moore, another British actor, raises glass and umbrella to wealth and comfort as he poses beside a gleaming Bentley in 1981, the year in which he starred with John Gielgud in the comedy *Arthur*.

Dudley Moore, otro actor británico, brinda por la riqueza y la comodidad delante de un reluciente Bentley en 1981, año en que protagonizó junto a John Gielgud la comedia *Arthur, el soltero de oro*.

Dudley Moore, un altro attore britannico, brinda alla bella vita davanti a una scintillante Bentley nel 1981, anno in cui a fianco di John Gielgud recita nella commedia *Arturo*.

Hot shot. Charlie Sheen, Brat Packer personified, recovers from forearm decoration in a tattoo parlour.

Una imagen *sexy*. Charlie Sheen, el mayor representante de la generación de actores denominada *Brat Pack* ("los niñatos"), se recupera después de decorarse el brazo en un estudio de tatuaje.

Hot shot. Charlie Sheen, uno dei principali esponenti del *Brat Pack*, alcuni momenti dopo essersi fatto tatuare l'avambraccio.

Cruise control. Tom Cruise, Brat Pack escapee and star of the 1986 action movie *Top Gun*.

Tom Cruise, fugitivo del Brat Pack y protagonista de la película de acción *Top Gun*, estrenada en 1986.

Tom Cruise, ex esponente del *Brat Pack* e star del film d'azione *Top Gun*, uscito nel 1986.

DAVID SILLITOE/THE GUARDIAN

He-man and
Herman. (Opposite)
Arnold Schwarzen-
egger in Conan the
Barbarian mode.
(Right) Paul Reubens
on the set of *Pee-
Wee's Playhouse*,
September 1986.

He-man y Herman.
(Página anterior)
Arnold Schwarze-
negger en una pose
típica de Conan el
Bárbaro. (Derecha)
Paul Reubens
durante el rodaje de
*La gran aventura de
Pee Wee*, septiembre
de 1986.

Il bel fusto e il
mingherlino. (Pagina
a fianco) Arnold
Schwarzenegger in
una posa stile Conan
il Barbaro. (A destra)
Paul Reubens sul set
di *Pee-Wee's
Playhouse*,
settembre 1986.

MARIO RUIZ/COLORIFIC!

DOUG MENUEZ/COLORIFIC!

Doris Day and Rock Hudson. A few weeks before his death from AIDS in
October 1985, Hudson spoke of his illness in a courageous attempt to draw
attention to the seriousness of the AIDS epidemic.

Doris Day y Rock Hudson. Poco antes de su muerte a causa del sida, acaecida
en octubre de 1985, Hudson habló abiertamente de su enfermedad: un valeroso
intento de concienciar a la opinión pública de la gravedad del sida.

Doris Day e Rock Hudson. Alcune settimane prima della sua morte per AIDS
nell'ottobre del 1985, Hudson parlò della sua malattia in un coraggioso
tentativo di attirare l'attenzione sulla gravità dell'AIDS.

Elizabeth Taylor at an AIDS Conference in the late 1980s. Throughout the 1980s, Taylor gave her support to the campaign against AIDS.

Elizabeth Taylor en una conferencia sobre el sida a finales de los años ochenta. A lo largo de la década, la actriz mostró su apoyo a la campaña contra la enfermedad.

Elizabeth Taylor in una conferenza sull'AIDS alla fine degli anni Ottanta. Per tutto il decennio, la famosa attrice appoggiò la campagna contro l'AIDS.

DENNIS BRACK/BLACK STAR/COLORIFIC!

6. The Arts
Las artes
Arte

Surrounded by his intricate graffiti-style designs, the American artist Keith Haring stares into the camera. One of his most celebrated works was a series of comical stick figures that decorated subway stations in New York. Haring died of AIDS in 1990.

El artista estadounidense Keith Haring mira directamente a la cámara, rodeado de sus intricados dibujos próximos al estilo del *graffiti*. Una de sus obras más célebres es una serie de siluetas cómicas que decora las estaciones del metro neoyorquino. Haring murió de sida en 1990.

Circondato dai suoi intricati disegni a mo' di graffiti, l'artista americano Keith Haring fissa con lo sguardo la macchina fotografica. Uno dei suoi lavori più celebri consisteva in una serie di silhouette comiche che decoravano le stazioni della metropolitana di New York. Haring morì di AIDS nel 1990.

6. The Arts
Las artes
Arte

European artists and art brokers cast their nets widely in the 1980s, turning for inspiration and profit to the art of Africa, Asia and South America. It was the age of multi-ethnic influence, a time when artists in New York, Paris and London borrowed from other, older civilisations. It was the age of multimedia presentation, exhibitions that featured video displays or linked works of art to gently humming computers. And it was the age of corporate sponsorship – after all, every new atrium needed its sculpted centre-piece.

The literary world was much enlivened by the death threat that hung over Salman Rushdie following the publication of *The Satanic Verses* in 1988. The book was banned and burned in India, and in Iran the Ayatollah Khomeini issued a *fatwa* against Rushdie the following year. A clutch of playwrights kept the straight theatre in good heart – David Mamet, Peter Shaffer, David Hare, Sam Shepard, Arthur Miller and many more. The stage musical plundered the history and geography syllabus for ever more unlikely subjects for a hit.

Los artistas y los marchantes de arte europeos ampliaron en los años ochenta su radio de acción y buscaron inspiración y beneficios en el arte de África, Asia y Sudamérica. Fue la era de la influencia multiétnica, una época en que los artistas de Nueva York, París y Londres volvieron la mirada hacia otras civilizaciones más antiguas. Fue también la era de las presentaciones multimedia, las exposiciones con imágenes de vídeo y la conexión de obras de arte a ordenadores, que las acompañaban con sus suaves zumbidos. Finalmente, fue la era del mecenazgo empresarial: al fin y al cabo, los vestíbulos de todas las empresas debían contar con la escultura de rigor.

El mundo literario saltó a la primera plana de los periódicos con la amenaza de muerte que pendió sobre Salman Rushdie tras la publicación de *Los versos satánicos* en 1988. Aquel año la obra fue prohibida y quemada en la India, y al año siguiente el ayatolá Jomeini lanzó una *fatwa* contra Rushdie en Irán. En cuanto al teatro de texto, un puñado de dramaturgos se encargaron de mantenerlo en buena forma (David Mamet, Peter Shaffer, David Hare, Sam Shepard y Arthur Miller, entre muchos otros), mientras que el teatro musical, por su parte, se dispuso a saquear los arcones de la historia y la geografía en busca de temas aún más insospechados con los que alcanzar el éxito.

Negli anni Ottanta, gli artisti ed i mercanti d'arte europei ampliarono i loro orizzonti, trovando una fonte di ispirazione e di profitto nell'arte africana, asiatica e sudamericana. Furono gli anni delle influenze multietniche, un periodo in cui gli artisti di New York, Parigi e Londra attinsero da altre civiltà più antiche. Era l'epoca delle presentazioni multimediali, delle esposizioni che mettevano in scena dei monitor e che associavano le opere d'arte a dei computer ronzanti. Ed era l'epoca della sponsorizzazione corporativa: alla fin fine, ogni nuova hall aveva bisogno della sua scultura come pezzo centrale.

Il mondo letterario venne scosso dalla minaccia di morte che incombeva su Salman Rushdie, in seguito alla pubblicazione de *I versetti satanici* nel 1988. Il libro venne proibito e messo al rogo in India, mentre in Iran, l'anno seguente, l'Ayatollah Khomeini emise una *fatwa* contro Rushdie. Nel teatro, un piccolo gruppo di drammaturghi si adoperavano per mantenere vivo il panorama teatrale, tra cui David Mamet, Peter Shaffer, David Hare, Sam Shepard, Arthur Miller e molti altri ancora. Il teatro musicale attingeva dalla storia e dalla geografia argomenti sempre più inverosimili, destinati ad essere dei grandi successi.

Gilbert Proesch and
George Passmore
(aka Gilbert and
George) pose in
front of yet another
self-made bid for
immortality,
July 1987.

Gilbert Proesch y
George Passmore
(alias Gilbert y
George) posan
delante de una
de sus obras: una
tentativa más de
inmortalidad, julio
de 1987.

Gilbert Proesch e
George Passmore
(alias Gilbert e
George) posano
di fronte a un loro
autoritratto,
l'ennesima sfida
all'immortalità,
luglio 1987.

DAVID KRYSZAK/BLACK STAR/COLORIFIC!

Art hit the streets and the walls as never before in the 1980s, bursting out of the studio and the gallery to decorate buses, trains, sheds, in fact any large flat surface. (Above) An artistic use of condoms for an AIDS billboard, August 1989.

En los años ochenta el arte irrumpió en las calles y sus muros como nunca lo había hecho, desbordando los estudios y las galerías de arte para decorar autobuses, trenes, naves industriales, y en realidad todas las superficies grandes y lisas. (Arriba) Un uso artístico del preservativo en una valla publicitaria de una campaña contra el sida, agosto de 1989.

Negli anni Ottanta, l'arte si impone nelle strade e sui muri come non aveva mai fatto prima, uscendo con impeto dagli studi e dalle gallerie per andare a decorare autobus, treni, capannoni e, di fatto, qualsiasi tipo di superficie ampia e piatta. (In alto) Un uso artistico dei preservativi per un cartellone sull'AIDS, agosto 1989.

NORMSKI/PYMCA

Graffiti reached the level of high art, with a discernible sense of style and a riotously rich use of colour. At its best, it brought at least momentary joy to dingy neighbourhoods. (Above) Old-school graffiti in Newcastle, 1985.

El *graffiti* se desarrolló al nivel de las bellas artes, con un estilo propio y un rico y atrevido uso del color. En los mejores casos, aportó una nota de alegría a los barrios más lúgubres. (Arriba) *Graffiti* de la vieja escuela en Newcastle, 1985.

I graffiti vennero innalzati al rango di vere e proprie opere d'arte, con un visibile senso dello stile ed un uso ricco e sfrenato del colore. Nel migliore dei casi, portarono almeno una certa gioia effimera nei quartieri più poveri. (In alto) Graffiti della vecchia scuola a Newcastle, 1985.

M GODDARD/COLORIFIC!

David Hockney, doyen of modern British painters, continued to spend most of his time in California throughout the 1980s. He turned increasingly to photography as an art form, hence the camera.

David Hockney, decano de los pintores británicos contemporáneos, siguió viviendo principalmente en California a lo largo de la década. Se interesó cada vez más por la fotografía; de ahí esta imagen del pintor con una cámara.

David Hockney, il decano dei pittori britannici moderni, passò gran parte del suo tempo in California durante il decennio degli anni Ottanta. Dimostrò un sempre maggiore interesse verso la fotografia come forma d'arte, da qui la macchina fotografica.

The graffiti artist, Jean-Michel Basquiat, New York City, 1980. Basquiat died from a heroin overdose in 1988 at the age of 27.

El artista del *graffiti* Jean-Michel Basquiat, Nueva York, 1980. Basquiat murió de sobredosis de heroína en 1988, a los 27 años de edad.

Il graffitista Jean-Michel Basquiat, New York, 1980. Basquiat morì di un'overdose di eroina nel 1988, all'età di 27 anni.

NAOKI OKAMOTO/BLACK STAR/COLORIFIC!

MARK CAFFERTY/BLACK STAR/COLORIFIC!

King of Kool and Prince of Pop. Jazz musician Miles Davis (left) and
Andy Warhol, 16 February 1987. Exactly one week later, Warhol died
after a gall bladder operation.

El rey del *kool* y el príncipe del *pop art*. El músico de *jazz* Miles Davis
(izquierda) junto a Andy Warhol, 16 de febrero de 1987. Justo una
semana después, Warhol murió como consecuencia de una intervención
quirúrgica de vesícula biliar.

Il re del Kool ed il principe della Pop Art. Il musicista jazz Miles Davis (a
sinistra) ed Andy Warhol, 16 febbraio 1987. Esattamente una settimana
dopo, Warhol morì in seguito ad un'operazione alla cistifellea.

American artist Julian Schnabel in his New York studio, December 1987. Behind him is a wall sculpture of broken plates.

El artista estadounidense Julian Schnabel en su estudio de Nueva York, diciembre de 1987. Detrás de él, una escultura mural elaborada con platos rotos.

L'artista americano Julian Schnabel nel suo studio di New York, dicembre 1987. Dietro di lui, una scultura su muro con frammenti di piatti incastonati.

BERNARD GOTFRYD/HULTON|ARCHIVE

Golden voices. Luciano Pavarotti (opposite) in a scene from the hugely unsuccessful MGM film *Yes, Giorgio*. (Above) The American soprano Jessye Norman, in a performance of *The Trojans*, 1983.

Voces de oro. Luciano Pavarotti (página anterior) en una escena de la película de la MGM *Sí, Giorgio*, un absoluto fracaso de taquilla. (Arriba) La soprano estadounidense Jessye Norman, durante una representación de *Los Troyanos*, 1983.

Voci d'oro. Luciano Pavarotti (pagina a fianco) in una scena tratta dallo sfortunato film della MGM *Yes, Giorgio*. (In alto) La soprano americana Jessye Norman, in una rappresentazione de *I Troiani*, 1983.

Mikhail Baryshnikov defies gravity as he performs *From Sea to Shining Sea*, New York City, 1981.

Mijail Baryshnikov desafía la ley de la gravedad en el espectáculo *From Sea to Shining Sea*, Nueva York, 1981.

Mikhail Baryshnikov sfida le leggi della gravità nello spettacolo intitolato *From Sea to Shining Sea*, New York, 1981.

The American dancer Jeffrey Daniels in costume for Andrew Lloyd Webber's stage musical *Starlight Express*, Apollo Theatre, London, 1980.

El bailarín estadounidense Jeffrey Daniels vestido para su papel en el musical de Andrew Lloyd Webber *Starlight Express*, Apollo Theatre, Londres, 1980.

Il ballerino americano Jeffrey Daniels, vestito per l'occasione, nel musical *Starlight Express* di Andrew Lloyd Webber, presso l'Apollo Theatre di Londra, 1980.

NEIL LIBBERT/THE OBSERVER/HULTON|ARCHIVE

The Twyla Tharp modern dance company performs the *Golden Section* from the ballet *The Catherine Wheel*, with a score by David Byrne of the new wave band Talking Heads, November 1983.

La compañía de danza contemporánea de Twyla Tharp interpreta *Golden Section*, del ballet *The Catherine Wheel*, con música de David Byrne, miembro del grupo de *new wave* Talking Heads, noviembre de 1983.

La compagnia di danza moderna Twyla Tharp interpreta *Golden Section*, tratto dal balletto *The Catherine Wheel*, con musiche di David Byrne, membro del gruppo new wave Talking Heads, novembre 1983.

The price of fame. Iranians support the *fatwa* and protest against Rushdie's book, Beirut 26 February 1989.

El precio de la fama. Iraníes apoyando la *fatwa* y manifestándose contra el libro de Rushdie, Beirut, 26 de febrero de 1989.

Il prezzo della fama. Gli iraniani sostengono la *fatwa* e si uniscono in protesta contro il libro di Rushdie, Beirut, 26 febbraio 1989.

The product of genius. Salman Rushdie with a copy of *The Satanic Verses*, the book that could have cost him his life, 17 February 1989.

La obra del genio. Salman Rushdie con un ejemplar de *Los versos satánicos*, el libro que pudo costarle la vida, 17 de febrero de 1989.

L'opera del genio. Salman Rushdie con una copia de *I Versetti satanici*, il libro che avrebbe potuto costargli la vita, 17 febbraio 1989.

NOBBY CLARK/THE OBSERVER/HULTON|ARCHIVE

American playwright, film writer and director David Mamet, 1985. Mamet's huge contribution to both stage and screen in the 1980s included *Glengarry Glen Ross* and *Speed the Plow*.

El dramaturgo, guionista y director estadounidense David Mamet, 1985. De la inmensa contribución de Mamet a los escenarios y la gran pantalla en los años ochenta destacan *Glengarry Glen Ross: éxito a cualquier precio* y *Speed the Plow*.

Il drammaturgo, sceneggiatore e regista americano David Mamet, 1985. Mamet diede il suo prolifico contributo al teatro ed al cinema durante gli anni Ottanta, con opere come *Glengarry Glen Ross* e *Speed the Plow*.

Sam Shepard, American dramatist and actor, with friend, November 1980. Shepard's major works in the 1980s included *Lie of the Mind* and the screenplay for the much acclaimed 1984 film *Paris, Texas.*

El dramaturgo y actor estadounidense Sam Shepard con un amigo, noviembre de 1980. Las grandes obras de Shepard en los años ochenta fueron *Lie of the Mind* y el guión de *París, Texas,* estrenada en 1984 con muy buena acogida.

L'americano Sam Shepard, drammaturgo ed attore, con il suo cane, novembre 1980. Tra le principali opere di Shepard nel corso degli anni Ottanta, si annoverano *Menzogne della mente* e la sceneggiatura del tanto acclamato film *Paris, Texas,* del 1984.

MELINDA WICKMAN/LIAISON AGENCY

Defying convention…
The English writer
and commentator
Quentin Crisp,
with his 37-year-
old gas stove,
Chelsea, London,
14 August 1981.

Desafiando las
convenciones…
El escritor y crítico
inglés Quentin Crisp,
con su vieja cocina
de gas de 37 años
de antigüedad, en
el barrio de Chelsea,
Londres, 14 de
agosto de 1981.

Sfidando le
convenzioni…
Lo scrittore e
commentatore
inglese Quentin
Crisp con la sua
cucina a gas,
comprata 37 anni
prima, Chelsea,
Londra, 14 agosto
1981.

IAN TYAS/KEYSTONE/HULTON|ARCHIVE

Tama Janowitz, author of *Slaves of New York*, takes time out from a Halloween party at the Salon des Artistes, SoHo, New York City, October 1987.

Tama Janowitz, autora de *Esclavos de Nueva York*, sale a tomar al aire en plena fiesta de Halloween en el Salon des Artistes, situado en el barrio del SoHo de Nueva York, octubre de 1987.

Tama Janowitz, autrice di *Slaves of New York*, prende il fresco all'uscita di una festa di Halloween, tenuta nel Salon des Artistes, nel quartiere di SoHo, a New York, ottobre 1987.

JEFFREY AARONSON/COLORIFIC!

Bold, brash, anti-establishment and highly idiosyncratic: American writer Hunter S Thompson, Aspen, Colorado. Thompson invented the style of subjective journalism he labelled 'Gonzo'.

Audaz, descarado, anti sistema y muy peculiar: el escritor estadounidense Hunter S. Thompson en Aspen, Colorado. Thompson inventó un estilo de periodismo subjetivo que bautizó como "Gonzo".

Audace, insolente, anti-establishment e veramente unico: lo scrittore americano Hunter S. Thompson, ad Aspen, Colorado. Thompson inventò uno stile di giornalismo soggettivo che lui stesso denominò "Gonzo".

William Burroughs,
one-time spokesman
for the 'Beat
Generation',
arrives in Madison,
Wisconsin, for a
reading from his
works, 1982.

William Burroughs,
antiguo portavoz de
la Beat Generation,
en Madison,
Wisconsin, con
motivo de una
lectura de sus obras,
1982.

Arrivo di William
Burroughs, allora
portavoce della
beat generation, a
Madison, Wisconsin,
per una lettura delle
sue opere, 1982.

JOE McNALLY/WHEELER/COLORIFIC!

ANTHONY SUAU/BLACK STAR/COLORIFIC!

Writer P J O'Rourke on the front line in South Korea, 1987. In the 1980s, O'Rourke
wrote for many magazines (including *Rolling Stone*, *Playboy* and *Esquire*) and also
published *Modern Manners* and *Republican Party Reptile*.

El escritor P. J. O'Rourke en primera línea en Corea del Sur, 1987. En los años ochenta,
O'Rourke escribió para muchas revistas (como *Rolling Stone*, *Playboy* y *Esquire*) y
publicó asimismo *Manual de malos modales* y *Alucinaciones de un reptil americano*.

Lo scrittore P. J. O'Rourke in prima linea in Corea del Sud, 1987. Negli anni Ottanta,
O'Rourke scrisse per molte riviste (*tra cui Rolling Stone*, *Playboy* ed *Esquire*) e pubblicò
anche *Modern Manners e Republican Party Reptile*.

The English novelist Martin Amis in the Portobello Road, Notting Hill, London, 1989. Amis drew much of his inspiration from the streets of London.

El novelista inglés Martin Amis en Portobello Road, Notting Hill, Londres, 1989. Amis tomó buena parte de su inspiración de las calles londinenses.

Il romanziere inglese Martin Amis a Portobello Road, Notting Hill, Londra, 1989. Amis trasse principalmente la sua ispirazione dalle strade di Londra.

MARK MORROW/BLACK STAR/COLORIFIC!

So little to do, so much time to do it... Tom Wolfe was less than prolific in the 1980s. He published only one novel – *The Bonfire of the Vanities* (1988) – but it was a huge success.

Muy poco que hacer y mucho tiempo para hacerlo... Tom Wolfe no fue precisamente un autor prolífico en los años ochenta. Publicó una sola novela, *La hoguera de las vanidades* (1988), pero fue un gran éxito.

Così poco da fare, così tanto tempo a disposizione... Tom Wolfe non fu affatto prolifico durante il decennio degli anni Ottanta. Pubblicò solo un romanzo, *Il falò delle vanità* (1988), grazie al quale, però, riscosse un gran successo.

HENRY GROSSMAN/COLORIFIC!

Death in the kitchen… American horror writer Stephen King brandishes a lobster, 1983. The knives on the wall may be for more than culinary purposes. King was perhaps the most commercially successful writer in the 1980s.

Muerte en la cocina… El novelista de terror estadounidense Stephen King empuñando una langosta, 1983. Los cuchillos de la pared tal vez tuvieran algo más que funciones culinarias. King fue quizá el autor con más éxito comercial de la década.

Morte in cucina… L'americano Stephen King, famoso scrittore di horror, brandisce un'aragosta, 1983. È possibile che i coltelli siano stati collocati sul muro a scopo non strettamente culinario. King è stato probabilmente lo scrittore che ha riscosso il più grande successo commerciale degli anni Ottanta.

7. Pop
La música pop
La musica pop

'It's like a jungle sometimes…' Pioneering rapper Grandmaster Flash and his Bronx-based group the Furious Five were the premier DJ-rap team of the early 1980s. These words, taken from his rap *The Message*, introduced rap's preoccupations: urban fear and loathing.

"A veces es como una jungla…" El pionero del *rap* Grandmaster Flash y su grupo del Bronx The Furious Five fueron el principal grupo de *disc-jockeys* de *rap* de principios de los años ochenta. La letra de su canción *The Message* dio paso al desarrollo de los temas característicos del género: el miedo y el odio urbanos.

"A volte sembra di essere in una giungla…" Il pioniere del rap Grandmaster Flash ed il suo gruppo del Bronx, i Furious Five, furono il primo gruppo DJ-rap degli inizi degli anni Ottanta. Queste parole, tratte dalla canzone *The Message*, riflettevano le preoccupazioni del rap: la paura urbana e l'odio.

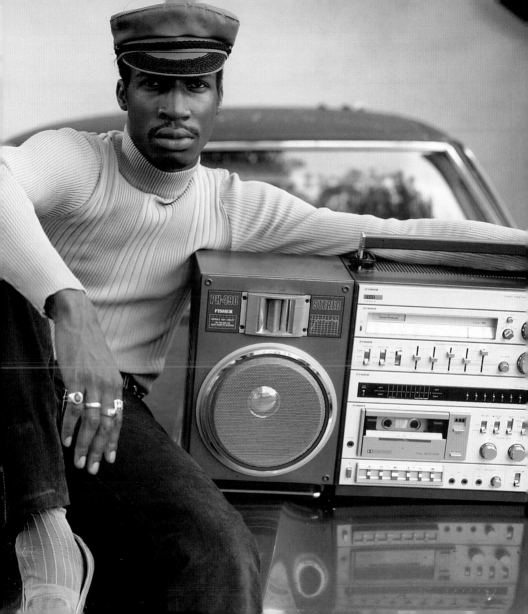

7. Pop
La música pop
La musica pop

The days of vinyl were numbered. Stocks of cassettes dwindled on the shelves of record stores but the introduction of the CD and the pop video was a shot in the arm for the music industry. Sales and profits spiralled; the incidence of fame and celebrity status reached all-time highs.

In Britain late in 1984, Band Aid released the single *Do They Know It's Christmas?* The £8 million proceeds from the sales of the single went to relieve starving millions in Ethiopia. In summer 1985 came the Global Jukebox, the simultaneous Live Aid concerts in Wembley Stadium, London and the JFK Stadium, Philadelphia. The concerts raised $70 million dollars, not enough alas to solve the worsening problems in even one corner of Africa. But it brought the world together, blazed a path through the jungle of pop, and awakened the consciences of pop stars for the rest of the century.

Apart from Band Aid/Live Aid, there were other things happening in music: electronic, New Romantic, Stock, Aitken and Waterman, Garage, hip hop/rap, Acid House – all had their place in the sun...

Los días del vinilo estaban contados. El número de casetes disminuía en las estanterías de las tiendas de discos, pero la introducción del disco compacto y del vídeo musical dieron savia nueva a la industria musical. Las ventas y los beneficios se dispararon; la importancia social de la fama y el estatus de los personajes famosos alcanzó máximos históricos.

Band Aid publicó a finales de 1984 el *single Do They Know It's Christmas?* en Gran Bretaña. Los ocho millones de libras de beneficios obtenidos en las ventas del *single* se destinaron a aliviar el hambre de millones de ciudadanos en Etiopía. En verano de 1985 se puso en marcha el proyecto Global Jukebox, consistente en dos conciertos simultáneos de Live Aid en el estadio Wembley de Londres y el estadio JFK de Filadelfia. Los conciertos recaudaron 70 millones de dólares, una cifra que por desgracia no bastó para resolver unos problemas acuciantes, ni siquiera en un pequeño rincón del continente africano, pero que unió al mundo, abrió una brecha en la jungla del pop y despertó la conciencia de las estrellas del pop durante lo que quedaba de siglo.

Además de Band Aid/Live Aid, pasaban otras cosas en el mundo de la música: la electrónica, los *New Romantics*, Stock, Aitken y Waterman, el *garage*, el *hip hop* y el *rap*, el *acid house*, etc.: todos tuvieron su hueco a lo largo de la década.

Il vinile aveva i giorni contati. Mentre gli stock di cassette diminuivano sugli scaffali dei negozi di musica, l'introduzione del CD e dei video pop rappresentò una boccata di ossigeno per l'industria della musica. Le vendite ed i profitti aumentavano vertiginosamente e la ripercussione della fama e della celebrità raggiunse il livello più alto di tutti i tempi.

Nel 1984, in Gran Bretagna, il Band Aid pubblicò il single *Do They Know It's Christmas?* Gli 8 milioni di sterline incassati dalle vendite del single vennero usati per soccorrere le vittime della fame in Etiopia. Nell'estate del 1985 fu la volta del Live Aid Global Jukebox, con i concerti simultanei nel Wembley Stadium di Londra e nel JFK Stadium di Philadelphia. I concerti incassarono 70 milioni di dollari, sfortunatamente non ancora sufficienti per risolvere i problemi sempre più gravi nemmeno in una piccola parte dell'Africa. Tuttavia, questa iniziativa solidale riuscì ad unire il mondo, aprendo una nuova via nella giungla del pop, e risvegliò la coscienza delle pop star per il resto del secolo.

Oltre al Band Aid ed al Live Aid, sorsero nuove correnti musicali tra cui l'elettronica, il New Romantic, il Garage, l'hip hop/rap e l'Acid House, così come grandi produttori e compositori, quali il gruppo "Stock, Aitken and Waterman". Ci fu un posto al sole per tutti.

DUNCAN RABAN/COLORIFIC!

(Left) The crowd at Wembley Stadium, London, for the Live Aid concert, 13 July 1985. (Above, left to right) George Michael, Bob Geldof and David Bowie.

(Izquierda) La multitud que llenó el estadio Wembley de Londres con motivo del concierto Live Aid, el 13 de julio de 1985. (Arriba, de izquierda a derecha) George Michael, Bob Geldof y David Bowie.

(A sinistra) La folla inonda lo stadio di Wembley, Londra, in occasione del concerto Live Aid, 13 luglio 1985. (In alto, da sinistra a destra) George Michael, Bob Geldof e David Bowie.

More Live Aid stars. Freddie Mercury with Queen at Wembley. The event raised $70 million for famine victims in Africa.

Más estrellas de Live Aid: Freddie Mercury con Queen en Wembley. Se recaudaron 70 millones de dólares en beneficio de las víctimas del hambre en África.

Altre star del Live Aid. Freddie Mercury con i Queen a Wembley. Il concerto raccolse 70 milioni di dollari da destinare al fondo per le vittime della fame in Africa.

Madonna getting into the groove at the Live Aid concert in Philadelphia, Pennsylvania, also on 13 July 1985.

Madonna *into the groove* en el concierto de Live Aid en Filadelfia, Pensilvania (Estados Unidos), celebrado también el 13 de julio de 1985.

Madonna canta scatenata al Live Aid di Philadelphia, Pennsylvania (USA), lo stesso 13 luglio del 1985.

FUNK/SIPA PRESS

Prince in his purple
period storms
through a number
from his hit film
and album of 1984,
Purple Rain.

Prince durante su
época púrpura
interpretando un
tema incluido en la
película y el álbum
Purple Rain, ambos
grandes éxitos en
1984.

Prince, nel suo
periodo "porpora",
interpreta con grinta
un brano tratto da
Purple Rain, film di
successo ed album
omonimo, usciti nel
1984.

Michael Jackson
on tour in London
following the release
of 1987's *Bad*. The
album generated five
separate Number 1
hits for him.

Actuación de
Michael Jackson
en Londres tras
la publicación
de su disco de
1987 *Bad*. El álbum
incluía cinco temas
que llegaron al
número 1 en las
listas.

Michael Jackson in
tournée a Londra,
dopo l'uscita
dell'album *Bad*, nel
1987. Questo album
gli fruttò ben cinque
n°1 nelle hit-parade.

The Stones roll
on and on… Mick
Jagger (left) with
Ron Wood, in
concert 1981.
'Everything going
on,' he said, 'I've
seen at least
twice before.'

Los Rolling Stones
siguen girando…
Mick Jagger
(izquierda) con
Ron Wood, en un
concierto de 1981.
"Todo lo que está
pasando lo he visto
como mínimo dos
veces", afirmó.

Gli Stones rotolano
e rotolano… Mick
Jagger (a sinistra) in
concerto con Ron
Wood, 1981. "Tutto
ciò che succede"
dichiarò "l'ho
già visto prima
perlomeno due
volte".

David Bowie
on tour with
Tin Machine,
1989. He formed
the band that year
with ex-Stooges
Tony and Hunt
Sales, and the
guitarist Reeves
Gabrels.

David Bowie de gira
con Tin Machine en
1989. Aquel año
formó una banda
con los ex miembros
de los Stooges Tony
y Hunt Sales, y el
guitarrista Reeves
Gabrels.

David Bowie in
tournée con i Tin
Machine, 1989.
Fondò il gruppo in
quell'anno con gli
ex-Stooges Tony ed
Hunt Sales, assieme
al chitarrista Reeves
Gabrels.

LESTER COHEN/SHOOTING STAR/COLORIFIC!

One of the biggest stars of the 1980s MTV era, Cyndi Lauper. Her huge hit *Girls Just Wanna Have Fun* later became the basis of several advertising campaigns.

Una de las mayores estrellas de la era MTV de los años ochenta, Cyndi Lauper. Su gran éxito *Girls Just Wanna Have Fun* se utilizó en varias campañas publicitarias.

Cyndi Lauper, una delle più grandi star dell'era MTV degli anni Ottanta. Il suo grande successo, *Girls Just Wanna Have Fun*, venne ripreso più tardi da numerose campagne pubblicitarie.

Whitney Houston, whose eponymous first album hit the charts at Number 1 and sold more than 14 million copies.

Whitney Houston, cuyo álbum de debut homónimo alcanzó el número 1 en las listas y vendió más de 14 millones de ejemplares.

Whitney Houston, il cui primo album eponimo raggiunse la vetta delle classifiche e vendette oltre 14 milioni di copie.

DIANA LYN/SHOOTING STAR/COLORIFIC!

Robert Palmer, the Dapper Dan of Eighties rock. His biggest success was *Addicted to Love*, from his 1985 solo album *Riptide*.

Robert Palmer, el hombre más elegante del rock de los años ochenta. Su mayor éxito fue *Addicted to Love*, extraído de su álbum en solitario *Riptide*, publicado en 1985.

Robert Palmer, il "Dapper Dan" del rock degli anni Ottanta. Il suo maggiore successo fu *Addicted to Love*, tratto dal suo album da solista *Riptide* (1985).

Dave Stewart (left)
and Annie Lennox
of the Eurythmics
spread the message
in their Katherine
Hamnett T-shirts
at Fashion Aid.

Dave Stewart
(izquierda) y
Annie Lennox,
componentes
de Eurythmics,
divulgan su mensaje
con camisetas de
Katherine Hamnett
en el espectáculo
benéfico Fashion
Aid.

Dave Stewart (a
sinistra) ed Annie
Lennox degli
Eurythmics
diffondono il
messaggio stampato
sulle magliette di
Katherine Hamnett,
al Fashion Aid.

DAVID LEVENSON/COLORIFIC!

COLORIFIC!

Marvin Lee Aday, aka Meat Loaf, gives his considerable all on stage in the
1980s. They were not good years for the superstar. After *Bad Attitude* and
Blind Before I Stop bombed, he filed for bankruptcy.

Marvin Lee Aday, conocido como Meat Loaf, da lo mucho que tiene que dar
de sí mismo en el escenario. No fue una buena época para esta superestrella.
Después de obtener sendos fracasos con *Bad Attitude* y *Blind Before I Stop*, se
declaró en quiebra.

Marvin Lee Aday, alias Meat Loaf, dà il meglio di sé sul palcoscenico. Gli
anni ottanta non furono troppo positivi per la superstar. Dopo il fiasco di *Bad
Attitude* e *Blind Before I Stop*, fu costretto a presentare un'istanza di fallimento.

The Boss comes home. Bruce Springsteen on stage in his home state, New Jersey, August 1985, the year of *Born in the USA.*

El Boss vuelve a casa. Bruce Springsteen en un escenario de su estado natal, Nueva Jersey, en agosto de 1985, el año de *Born in the USA.*

Il Boss ritorna a casa. Bruce Springsteen sul palcoscenico nel suo stato natale, New Jersey, agosto 1985, l'anno di *Born in the USA.*

FRATKIN/SIPA PRESS

HONEY SALVADORI/COLORIFIC!

The joys of touring... Luke and Matt Goss greet the dawn in the comfort of their limousine, 1989.

La diversión de las giras... Luke y Matt Goss saludan al amanecer en su confortable limusina, 1989.

Le gioie della vita in tournée... Luke e Matt Goss salutano il nuovo giorno nel comfort della loro limousine, 1989.

TONY MOTT/S.I.N.

They evolved in the world-weary late 1970s with a cover version of *Satisfaction* they sang wearing industrial cleaning outfits, but Devo (above) believed that the world was de-evolving into increasingly dysfunctional societies.

Triunfaron en un mundo consumido por el hastío a finales de los años setenta, con una versión de *Satisfaction* y sus uniformes de trabajo. Los componentes de Devo (arriba) creían que el mundo estaba en plena degeneración y producía sociedades cada vez más disfuncionales.

Si evolsero nel mondo tedioso degli ultimi anni Settanta con una cover di *Satisfaction*, che cantavano indossando delle tute da lavoro blu. Secondo Devo (in alto), il mondo stava subendo un'involuzione verso una società sempre più disfunzionale.

KATIA NATOZA/S.I.N.

Less cynical and more melodic were Bon Jovi (above), led by Jon Bon Jovi (centre). Combining mainstream hard rock with metal, the band had great success with *Slippery When Wet* (1986) and *New Jersey* (1988).

Menos cínicos y más melódicos eran Bon Jovi (arriba), liderados por Jon Bon Jovi (centro). Mezclando el *hard rock* más accesible con el *heavy metal*, el grupo consiguió grandes éxitos con los discos *Slippery When Wet* (1986) y *New Jersey* (1988).

Meno cinici e più melodici furono i Bon Jovi (in alto), capeggiati da Jon Bon Jovi (al centro). Combinando l'hard rock rivolto al grande pubblico con il metal, il gruppo riscosse un grande successo con *Slippery When Wet* (1986) e *New Jersey* (1988).

TERENCE SPENCER/COLORIFIC!

(Above) The Police on set for their video single *Synchronicity* (1983) – (left to right) Andy Summers, Sting and Stewart Copeland. (Opposite) Duran Duran pose for a still while filming their video *Wild Boys* (1984).

(Arriba) Police durante la grabación del vídeo musical del *single Synchronicity* (1983): (de izquierda a derecha) Andy Summers, Sting y Stewart Copeland. (Página siguiente) Los Duran Duran posan para una fotografía durante el rodaje del videoclip de *Wild Boys* (1984).

(In alto) I Police sul set del video del loro single *Synchronicity* (1983) – (da sinistra a destra) Andy Summers, Sting e Stewart Copeland. (Pagina a fianco) I Duran Duran posano per una foto durante la registrazione del video *Wild Boys* (1984).

Straight outta Compton. South Central LA
rapper Ice-T starts the body count on stage
in London, 1989.

Directamente desde Compton. El rapero
Ice-T, originario del barrio de South
Central de Los Ángeles, en un concierto
en Londres, 1989.

Direttamente da Compton. Ice-T, il rapper
del distretto di South Central di Los Angeles,
inizia il "conteggio dei corpi" su un
palcoscenico londinese, 1989.

Chuck D (fist clenched) and Flavor Flav (front, centre) of Public Enemy 'bum rush' the show at the Apollo, Manchester, 1989.

Chuck D (con el puño cerrado) y Flavor Flav (delante, centro) de Public Enemy animan al público durante su actuación en la sala Apollo de Manchester en 1989.

Chuck D (con il pugno stretto) e Flavor Flav (davanti, al centro) dei Public Enemy scaldano la folla all'Apollo, Manchester, 1989.

NORMSKI/PYMCA

(Left to right) Flavor Flav, LL Cool J and DJ Bobcat. LL's knack for making hip hop accessible led to accusations of selling out. Later he successfully turned his career to film and television.

(De izquierda a derecha) Flavor Flav, LL Cool J y DJ Bobcat. Por su habilidad para hacer accesible el *hip hop*, LL Cool J fue acusado de venderse. Posteriormente inició una exitosa carrera en el cine y la televisión.

(Da sinistra a destra) Flavor Flav, LL Cool J e DJ Bobcat. Per la sua capacità di rendere l'hip hop accessibile a tutti, LL venne accusato di essersi venduto. Più tardi, indirizzò con successo la sua carriera verso il mondo del cinema e della televisione.

Getting his shirt
lifted, Morrissey
sings on with
The Smiths
at a gig at the
Liverpool
Corn Exhange,
February 1986.

Morrissey se deja
quitar la camisa
mientras canta
junto con su grupo
The Smiths en la
sala Liverpool Corn
Exhange, febrero
de 1986.

Durante
un'esibizione
insieme agli Smiths,
al Liverpool Corn
Exhange, il pubblico
gli solleva la camicia
ma Morrissey
continua a cantare
imperterrito,
febbraio 1986.

Friends and admirers. (Left) Steve Strange prays outside the gates of the Hell club, 1980. Ahead lay success, rather than damnation, with *Fade to Grey*.

Amigos y admiradores. (Izquierda) Steve Strange reza delante de la puerta del club Hell, 1980. No le esperaba la condenación, sino el éxito con su trabajo *Fade to Grey*.

Amici ed ammiratori. (A sinistra) Steve Strange prega davanti all'ingresso del club *Hell* (inferno), 1980. Poco più tardi, sarebbe seguito il successo, piuttosto che la dannazione, con *Fade to Grey*.

Boy George outside
the entrance to
Le Beat Route club,
Soho, London,
1981. Ahead lay
success with Culture
Club's *Do You
Really Want to
Hurt Me?*

Boy George delante
de la entrada del
club Le Beat Route,
Soho, Londres,
1981. Le esperaba el
éxito con la canción
de Culture Club *Do
You Really Want to
Hurt Me?*

Boy George fuori
dall'entrata del *Le
Beat Route club*,
Soho, Londra, 1981.
Il successo non si
fece aspettare: arrivò
con *Do You Really
Want to Hurt Me?*
dei Culture Club.

DEREK RIDGERS/PYMCA

Australian singer, songwriter and novelist Nick Cave, founder and leader of the Bad Seeds, in introspective mood, 1985.

El cantautor y novelista Nick Cave, fundador y líder de los Bad Seeds, en un momento introspectivo, 1985.

Il cantante, compositore e romanziere australiano Nick Cave, fondatore e leader del gruppo Bad Seeds, in un atteggiamento introspettivo, 1985.

PETER ANDERSON/S.I.N.

Adam Ant applies war paint before going on stage, 1981. It was the year of *Stand and Deliver* and *Prince Charming*.

Adam Ant se aplica pinturas de guerra antes de subir al escenario, 1981. Fue el año de *Stand and Deliver* y *Prince Charming*.

Adam Ant si pittura la faccia come un guerriero prima di salire sul palco, 1981. Era l'anno di *Stand and Deliver* e *Prince Charming*.

IAN TILTON/S.I.N.

Robert Smith, leader of The Cure, in typically ghoulish mode, though without his trademark lipstick smudge.

Robert Smith, líder de The Cure, con su habitual aspecto macabro, aunque sin su típico pintalabios corrido.

Robert Smith, leader dei Cure, con il suo particolare aspetto sinistro, ma senza il suo tipico rossetto sbavato.

Siouxsie Sioux
of Siouxsie and the
Banshees, one of
the longest lasting
of the 1970s-
spawned punk
bands.

Siouxsie Sioux,
cantante de Siouxsie
and the Banshees,
uno de los grupos
punk de los años
setenta que siguió
en activo varios
años más.

Siouxsie Sioux
dei *Siouxsie and
the Banshees*, uno
dei gruppi punk
più longevi tra
quelli sorti negli
anni Settanta.

PETER ANDERSON/S.I.N.

8. Fashion
Moda
Moda

Princess Diana steps out at the British première of Robert Zemeckis's *Back to the Future*, 1985. By this time she had abandoned her Sloane Ranger look for a far more sophisticated wardrobe.

La princesa Diana a la salida del estreno en Gran Bretaña de la película de Robert Zemeckis *Regreso al futuro*, en 1985. Ya había abandonado su estilo de "niña bien" y vestía de forma mucho más refinada.

La Principessa Diana all'uscita dalla prima britannica del film di Robert Zemeckis *Ritorno al futuro* (1985). All'epoca Diana aveva già abbandonato il suo look "Sloane Ranger" (campagnolo e caro al tempo stesso) per uno molto più sofisticato.

8. Fashion
Moda
Moda

Whereas the Seventies had their fashion trademarks in the mini and the punk, no particular style typified the 1980s. Instead, they had an icon – Diana, Princess of Wales. Shy and jejune when she first appeared towards the end of the 1970s, by the time she married Prince Charles in July 1981 Diana (and her wedding dress) had captured the imagination of women everywhere. By the end of the decade, her style and influence had spread all over the world.

In the fashion houses there were few changes. The established names – Courrèges, Saint Laurent, Gucci, Armani, Westwood, Lagerfeld and a dozen more – still held sway over the catwalks of Paris, Milan, New York and London. But there were also relative newcomers, among them Katharine Hamnett, Christian Lacroix, Caroline Charles and, at the forefront of Japanese designers, Issey Miyake and Comme des Garçons.

Meanwhile, out on the streets, fashions continued to mutate and became harder to pin down. The Doc Marten boot, that old stand-by of the Seventies, was given high-fashion status on the catwalk before it returned to the street as a shoe.

La moda de los años setenta se caracterizó por prendas como la minifalda y por el estilo *punk*, pero los ochenta no se definieron por un estilo concreto, sino por un icono: Diana, princesa de Gales. En sus primeras apariciones a finales de los años setenta tenía un aspecto tímido e ingenuo, pero en la ceremonia de boda con el príncipe Carlos de Inglaterra, en julio de 1981, sedujo con su vestido a mujeres de todo el planeta. A finales de la década, su estilo y su influencia se habían extendido por todo el mundo.

En las grandes firmas de la moda hubo pocos cambios. Los nombres establecidos –Courrèges, Saint Laurent, Gucci, Armani, Westwood, Lagerfeld y algunos más–

siguieron reinando en las pasarelas de París, Milán, Nueva York y Londres. Pero también hubo nuevos nombres, como los de Katharine Hamnett, Christian Lacroix, Caroline Charles y, en primera línea de los diseñadores japoneses, Issey Miyake y Comme des Garçons.

Mientras tanto, en la calle, la moda seguía trasformándose y se hizo más difícil de definir. Las botas Doc Marten, una herencia de los años setenta, entraron en la alta costura y finalmente volvieron a la calle en versión zapato.

Mentre negli anni Settanta i segni distintivi del settore della moda erano stati la minigonna e il punk, gli anni Ottanta non si caratterizzarono per nessuno stile particolare. Ebbero invece un'icona di riferimento – Diana, la principessa del Galles. Timida e ingenua alla sua prima apparizione verso la fine degli anni Settanta, prima che sposasse il principe Carlo nel luglio del 1981, Diana (e il suo abito da sposa) avevano catturato ovunque l'attenzione delle donne. Prima della fine del decennio, il suo stile era copiato in tutto il mondo.

Nelle grandi case della moda, vi furono pochi cambiamenti. I nomi già affermati – Courrèges, Saint Laurent, Gucci, Armani, Westwood, Lagerfeld e molti altri – padroneggiavano ancora sulle passerelle di Parigi, Milano, New York e Londra. Ma c'erano anche dei volti relativamente nuovi, tra cui Katharine Hamnett, Christian Lacroix, Caroline Charles e, all'avanguardia degli stilisti giapponesi, Issey Miyake e Comme des Garçons.

Nel frattempo, in strada, la moda continuava a cambiare ed era sempre più difficile identificare chiaramente i vari stili. Gli anfibi Dr. Marten's, un vecchio accessorio degli anni Settanta, erano diventati un oggetto di alta moda sulle passerelle prima di ritornare in strada e riacquisire lo status di semplici scarpe.

A glum Diana visits a Huddersfield youth centre, 22 March 1982. That cup of tea proves to be a useless fashion accessory.

La princesa Diana, con aspecto decaído, en una visita a un centro juvenil de Huddersfield, el 22 de marzo de 1982. La taza de té no sirve como accesorio de moda.

Una Diana un po' abbacchiata visita un centro giovanile di Huddersfield, 22 marzo 1982. Quella tazza di tè si rivela un accessorio di moda alquanto superfluo.

KEYSTONE/HULTON|ARCHIVE

Power dressing, royal style… Diana at a wedding in 1983. Neither her mother-in-law nor her sister-in-law could match such swagger.

Vestida para triunfar, en el seno de la realeza… Diana en una boda en 1983. Ni su suegra ni su cuñada la igualaban en distinción.

Abbigliamento efficiente e fiducioso, stile reale… Diana a un matrimonio nel 1983. Né sua suocera né sua cognata poterono uguagliare tale elegante portamento.

Giorgio Armani,
1987. Although
Armani was big
on wide, padded
shoulders, they
were never as
big as the coat-
hanger suggests.

Giorgio Armani,
1987. Armani era
partidario de los
hombros anchos
con hombreras,
pero nunca llegó a
las dimensiones de
esta percha.

Giorgio Armani,
1987. Sebbene
Armani amasse
tantissimo le spalle
larghe e imbottite,
queste non erano
mai tanto grandi
quanto il loro
appendiabiti
potrebbe far
pensare.

Gianni Versace and dummy at home on Lake Como, June 1983. Those looking for subtlety and minimalism would not find them in Versace's designs.

Gianni Versace con un maniquí en su casa del lago de Como, junio de 1983. Los partidarios de la sutileza y el minimalismo no hubieran encontrado su estilo en los diseños de Versace.

Gianni Versace accanto a un manichino nella sua casa sul lago di Como, giugno 1983. Chi cercava finezza e minimalismo non li avrebbe trovati nei disegni di Versace.

Issey Miyake proves the truth of Coco Chanel's claim that 'fashion is architecture' with this heavy item of knitwear, 1982.

Issey Miyake demuestra con este enorme jersey que Coco Chanel estaba en lo cierto cuando dijo que "la moda es arquitectura", 1982.

Con questo pesante capo fatto a maglia, Issey Miyake dimostra che Coco Chanel aveva ragione quando affermò che "la moda è architettura" 1982.

Some designs created by Miyake (right) were mounted on sculptural wire that allowed them to stand out from the body.

Algunos diseños de Miyake (derecha) incorporaban una malla metálica que separaba la ropa del cuerpo.

Alcuni disegni creati da Miyake (a destra) venivano montati su delle strutture fatte in fil di ferro in modo tale da farli spiccare e staccare dal corpo.

EIJI MIYAZAWA/BLACK STAR/COLORIFIC!

Model turned
actress Lauren
Hutton adopts a rich
disco look for the
1980 Academy
Awards ceremony,
Los Angeles.

La ex modelo y
actriz Lauren
Hutton adopta
una deslumbrante
imagen *disco* para
la ceremonia de los
oscars de 1980 en
Los Ángeles.

La modella diventata
attrice Lauren
Hutton adotta
un vistoso look
da discoteca per
la cerimonia degli
Oscar, Los Angeles,
1980.

Michelle Pfeiffer as she appeared in the 1983 Brian de Palma movie *Scarface*. For some reason, Pfeiffer thought she had a face like a duck.

Michelle Pfeiffer, tal y como apareció en la película de Brian de Palma *El precio del poder,* estrenada en 1983. Por algún motivo, Pfeiffer creía que tenía cara de pato.

Michelle Pfeiffer come appariva nel film di Brian de Palma *Scarface*, 1983. Per qualche motivo, Pfeiffer pensava di avere una faccia da anatra.

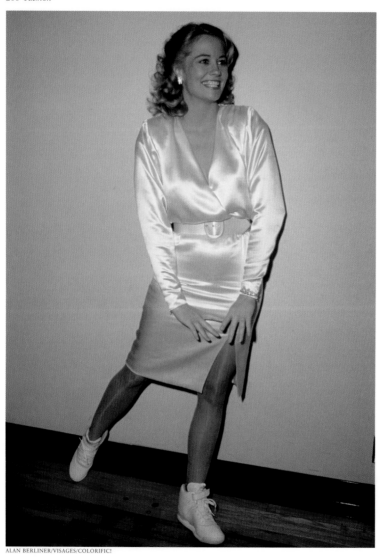

Couture meets casual. Cybil Shepherd, star of TV's *Moonlighting*, wears trainers with an evening dress. Nice.

Alta costura e imagen informal. Cybil Shepherd, protagonista de la serie de televisión *Luz de luna*, con zapatillas deportivas y vestido de noche. Una combinación perfecta.

Elegante e al contempo casual. Cybil Shepherd, star delle serie televisiva *Moonlighting*, indossa delle scarpe da ginnastica con un abito da sera. Carina.

A stone-washed, pre-ripped, *Footloose* Sarah Jessica Parker just wanted to have fun.

Sarah Jessica Parker, de *Footloose,* con tejanos lavados a la piedra rotos. Como decía Cindy Lauper, solo quería divertirse.

Un look slavato, stracciato, per Sarah Jessica Parker di *Footloose*, che voleva solo divertirsi.

DIANA LYN/SHOOTING STAR/COLORIFIC!

The leisurewear fashion. Jamie Lee Curtis in work-out mode for the 1985 James Bridges film *Perfect*.

Moda deportiva. Jamie Lee Curtis entrenándose para el largometraje de 1985 *Perfect*, dirigido por James Bridges.

La moda dell'abbigliamento sportivo-informale. Jamie Lee Curtis in tenuta da allenamento per il film di James Bridges *Perfect*, del 1985.

COLOMBIA PICTURES/HULTON|ARCHIVE

Linda Evans, soapy star of the 1980s TV hit *Dynasty*, in obligatory headband, leotard and leggings at her private gym, 1983.

Linda Evans, protagonista de la exitosa teleserie de los ochenta *Dinastía* en su gimnasio privado, vestida con el uniforme obligatorio: cinta en el pelo, mallas y calentadores, 1983.

Linda Evans, sdolcinata star di *Dynasty*, serie TV di successo degli Ottanta, posa nella sua palestra privata in perfetta mise sportiva: fascia tergisudore, body aderente e fuseaux, 1983.

Madonna in concert, 1985. Her studied 'couldn't care less' look was widely copied.

Madonna en concierto, 1985. Su estudiada imagen descuidada fue muy imitada.

Madonna in concerto, 1985. Il suo look spensierato fu imitato moltissimo.

RODRIGUEZ/LIAISON AGENCY

Madonna gave wannabes a look to follow for a year or so, one characterised by trousers or mini skirt, lacy tops, necklaces and oversized knitwear. The look offered liberation without stigma.

Madonna ofreció a sus fans durante aproximadamente un año un estilo con el que identificarse, caracterizado por pantalones o minifalda, camisetas de encaje, collares y jerseys enormes. Era un estilo liberador y desinhibido.

Madonna propose ai suoi emuli e fedeli fan un look che durò per una stagione o poco più, caratterizzato da pantaloni o minigonne, top in pizzo, collane e indumenti a maglia fuori misura. Era un look che offriva libertà senza però essere scandaloso.

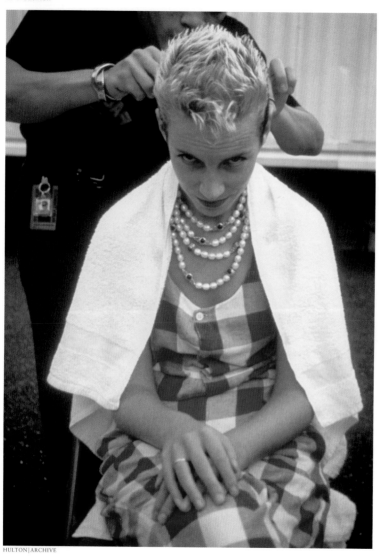

Annie Lennox gets
her Eurythmics crop
renewed for the
Sweet Dreams
Tour of 1983–4.

Annie Lennox en
la peluquería,
arreglándose su
clásico peinado
Eurythmics para la
gira Sweet Dreams
(1983–1984).

Acconciatura
decisamente corta
per Annie Lennox
in vista del Tour
1983-4 degli
Eurythmics
intitolato
Sweet Dreams.

Blonde with ambition. By 1986 Madonna had changed her image yet again: this was the way she looked on the cover of *True Blue*.

Rubia y ambiciosa. En 1986 Madonna volvió a cambiar de imagen: en la fotografía, su *look* para la portada del disco *True Blue*.

Ambizione bionda. Nel 1986 Madonna cambia ancora una volta la sua immagine: questo è il look scelto per la foto di copertina dell'album *True Blue*.

JOHN REARDON/THE OBSERVER/HULTON|ARCHIVE

Punk was reborn in the mid-Eighties as a big bold (commercial) fashion statement. In the King's Road, punks now charged for their photographs to be taken. (Above) Two punks in London's Hyde Park, 26 October 1986.

El *punk* resurgió a mediados de los años ochenta como una moda atrevida, pero comercial. En la calle londinense de King's Road los *punks* cobraban a quien les quería hacer fotografías. (Arriba) Dos *punks* en el Hyde Park de Londres, 26 de octubre de 1986.

Verso la metà degli anni Ottanta si assistette al grande e spavaldo ritorno in termini di moda (ed anche commerciali) dello stile punk. A King's Road, i punk si facevano pagare per farsi fotografare. (In alto) Due punk a Hyde Park, Londra, 26 ottobre 1986.

The African-American 'cornrow' braided hairstyle gained fleeting popularity, thanks to Bo Derek and the 1980 film *10*.

Las trenzas de estilo afroamericano tuvieron una fugaz popularidad, gracias a Bo Derek y su película de 1980 *Diez, la mujer perfecta*.

Successo di breve durata per l'acconciatura in stile afroamericano, con treccine intrecciate a perline, resa popolare da Bo Derek nel film del 1980 *10*.

BERNARD GOTFRYD/HULTON|ARCHIVE

A metalhead at
London's
Hammersmith
Odeon, 1981, the
mecca for heavy
metal fans in
the Eighties.

Una fan del *heavy
metal* en la sala
de conciertos
londinense
Hammersmith
Odeon, la meca del
género durante la
década, 1981.

1981, una metallara
all' Hammersmith
Odeon di Londra,
negli anni Ottanta
la mecca per i fan
dell'heavy metal.

LL Cool J says it all with beanie, dukie chain and bomber jacket at a Def Jam party, London, 1987.

LL Cool J expresa su credo con su gorro, una cadena y una chaqueta de aviador en una fiesta del sello discográfico Def Jam, Londres, 1987.

LL Cool J sfoggia bomber, catena d'oro e cappellino rotondo durante un'esibizione al Def Jam, Londra, 1987.

Early rave fashions
of 1988. The outfits
are a meeting of
post-Culture Club
and up-and-coming
Acid House.

Primeros ejemplos
del estilo
característico de las
fiestas *rave*, 1988.
En estos atuendos se
mezcla el estilo post
"cultura de clubs" y
el del emergente
acid house.

I primi presagi della
moda rave nel 1988.
Gli abiti nascono
dall'incontro di
due stili: quello
post-Culture Club
e l'emergente Acid
House.

Punk shows its
softer side with
mohair jumper
and jeans, 1986.
Knitwear made
a considerable
comeback in
the 1980s.

El *punk* mostrando
su lado más suave
con un jersey de
mohair y unos
tejanos, 1986.
Los jerseys de lana
resurgieron con
fuerza en la década
de los ochenta.

I punk mostrano il
loro lato più tenero
indossando maglioni
di mohair e jeans,
1986. Negli anni
Ottanta gli abiti a
maglia ritornarono
in auge.

TED POLHEMUS/PYMCA

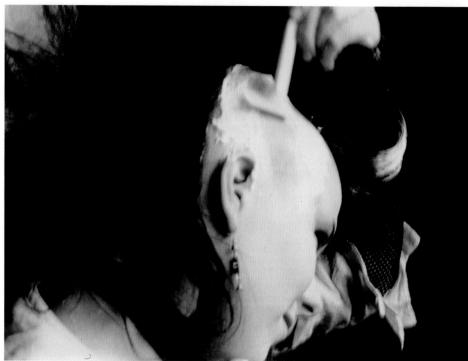

GAVIN WATSON/PYMCA

The dark side emerges with new variations on anti-fashion fashion. (Above) An aspiring trend-setter indulges in a do-it-yourself Mohican hair cut as part of a punk-Goth transformation.

La imagen oscura resurge con nuevas variaciones contrarias a la moda establecida. (Arriba) Una aspirante a apóstol de la moda se corta el pelo a lo mohicano, un rasgo característico del paso del *punk* al estilo gótico.

Nel settore della moda anti-moda emerge il lato oscuro con nuove varianti. (In alto) Un aspirante creatore di tendenze esegue un taglio da moicano "fai da te" come parte di una trasformazione punk-gotica.

TED POLHEMUS/PYMCA

An end to such old-fashioned concerns as 'are my seams straight?' and 'does my bum look big in this?'. Flesh bursts through the ladders that led to fashion success in the world of Goth.

Se acabaron viejas preocupaciones como "¿llevo las costuras rectas?" y "¿me hace el culo gordo?". En la imagen, la piel desborda las carreras de las medias, una característica del estilo gótico que contribuyó a su éxito popular.

Sono ormai finiti i tempi di preoccupazioni antiquate del tipo: "sono dritte le cuciture delle mie calze?" e "quest'abito mi fa il sedere grosso?". La carne irrompe tra le smagliature, trasformatesi poi in elemento di successo della moda gotica.

9. Youth
La juventud
Giovani

The ultimate in street smartness – against a wall of graffiti, young males gather for a breakdancing session, 1984. Athletic, dazzlingly brilliant, slightly dangerous, above all it was something that adults simply couldn't do.

El colmo del estilo urbano: frente a un muro cubierto de *graffiti*, un grupo de chicos se reúne para una sesión de *breakdance,* 1984. Era una actividad atlética, espectacular, algo peligrosa y, sobre todo, imposible de practicar para los adultos.

L'ultimo grido della moda di strada – giovani riuniti per una sessione di breakdance davanti ad una parete coperta di graffiti, 1984. Una performance atletica, frenetica e un poco pericolosa ma, soprattutto, qualcosa che gli adulti non sarebbero riusciti a fare.

9. Youth
La juventud
Giovani

The trend towards establishing a separate youth culture that had started in the 1950s and had come on stream in the 1960s reached full flood in the 1980s. Young people had more money and fewer inhibitions. They worked hard and played hard. Perhaps the planet was in need of care and attention, but, right now, life was for the energetic and youth had enough energy to light up the world.

East and west, every major city had its club scene. Lights flashed, pills popped, liquor was consumed in enormous quantities, people collapsed, some even died, but the beat and the dance and the fun went on, wiping out the rest of the weekend but allowing those with jobs to creep back to work in the cruel light of Monday morning.

On streets where children once cavorted, youth now exhibited their skills as skateboarders, rollerbladers or breakdancers, took their ghetto-blasters for a walk, or simply passed the time. In doorways and derelict buildings, alleys and passageways, there were those who nursed their ever-dwindling stocks of drugs and wondered where the next hit was coming from.

El camino hacia una cultura juvenil independiente, iniciado en los años cincuenta y desarrollado en el transcurso de los sesenta, vivió una auténtica explosión en los ochenta. A lo largo de la década, los jóvenes tuvieron más dinero y menos complejos. Trabajaban mucho y apostaban fuerte. Muy probablemente, el planeta necesitaba cuidado y atenciones, pero, por el momento, la vida era para quienes tenían energía, y los jóvenes tenían energía suficiente para hacer avanzar el mundo.

En Oriente y Occidente, todas las grandes ciudades tenían sus discotecas. Las luces brillaban, aparecieron las pastillas, se consumía alcohol en cantidades inmensas, se perdía la conciencia y a veces incluso la vida, pero el ritmo, el baile y la diversión seguían. Daba igual que el resto del fin de semana pasara como una exhalación: quienes trabajaban siempre podían volver a rastras a su puesto bajo el cruel sol del lunes por la mañana.

En las calles donde hasta hacía poco jugaban los niños, ahora los jóvenes exhibían su habilidad con el monopatín, los patines o como bailarines de *breakdance;* se iban a dar una vuelta con el radiocasete apoyado en el hombro o sencillamente pasaban el rato. Y en puertas y edificios abandonados, en pasajes y callejones, los consumidores de drogas se preguntaban dónde encontrarían la siguiente dosis.

La tendenza verso la creazione di una cultura giovanile, che era iniziata negli anni Cinquanta e aveva preso corpo negli anni Sessanta, s'impose del tutto durante gli anni Ottanta. I giovani disponevano di una maggior quantità di denaro ed erano meno inibiti. Lavoravano e giocavano duro. Il pianeta poteva anche avere bisogno di cure e attenzioni ma, per il momento, la vita apparteneva a chi era pieno d'energia, e i giovani, di energia, ne avevano abbastanza da illuminare il mondo.

A est e ad ovest, tutte le città più importanti avevano una loro vita notturna. Le luci brillavano, le droghe circolavano e venivano consumate enormi quantità di alcol; alcuni crollavano, altri addirittura morivano, ma il ritmo, i balli e il divertimento continuavano fino ad esaurire ciò che restava del fine settimana. E tuttavia, chi aveva un impiego riusciva ancora a trascinarsi al lavoro alla luce spietata del lunedì mattina.

Nelle strade dove una volta giocavano e saltavano i bambini, i giovani mostravano ora la propria abilità sullo skateboard e sui rollerblade o come ballerini di breakdance, andavano in giro con degli enormi radioregistratori o, semplicemente, passavano il tempo. Nei portoni e negli edifici abbandonati, nei vicoli e nei passaggi, sostava chi vedeva scemare le proprie riserve di droga, chiedendosi da dove sarebbe venuta la prossima dose.

BILL BERNSTEIN/BLACK STAR/COLORIFIC!

Dancing lay at the centre of a great deal of social life and leisure time
for many young people. (Above) Dancers hit the floor at the re-opening
of Studio 54 in New York City, 15 September 1981.

El baile era una actividad básica en la vida social y el ocio de muchos
jóvenes. (Arriba) Los asistentes a la reinauguración de la discoteca
neoyorquina Studio 54 saltan a la pista, 15 de septiembre de 1981.

Per molti giovani, il ballo costituiva il fulcro della vita sociale e del tempo
libero. (In alto) Ballerini scatenati alla riapertura dello Studio 54 di New
York, 15 settembre 1981.

The joys and jewels of Studio 54 are proudly displayed by a metallic painted dancer on opening night.

En la inauguración de Studio 54 un bailarín embadurnado con pintura metálica exhibe con orgullo los placeres y los tesoros que se hallaban en el interior de la discoteca.

Un ballerino truccato con vernice metallizzata esibisce orgoglioso i piaceri e le gioie dello Studio 54 la notte dell'apertura.

TOM GATES/HULTON|ARCHIVO

DAVID SWINDELLS/PYMCA

Oh, my America. Two neo-naturists take to the floor for a rave celebrating American Independence Day at Taboo, 218 East 52nd Street, New York City, 4 July 1985.

¡América! Dos neonaturistas invaden la pista en una *rave* en conmemoración del día de la independencia de Estados Unidos en Taboo, calle 52 Este, 218, Nueva York, 4 de julio de 1985.

America, America! Due neo-naturiste scendono in pista in occasione di una scatenata celebrazione dell'anniversario dell'indipendenza presso il Taboo, 218 East 52nd Street, New York, 4 luglio 1985.

Not an optical illusion but a performance by David Cabaret at Pyramid at Heaven, London, 1987.

No se trata de una ilusión óptica, sino de una *performance* de David Cabaret en el club Pyramid at Heaven, Londres, 1987.

Non è un'illusione ottica: è una performance di David Cabaret al Pyramid at Heaven, Londra, 1987.

DAVID SWINDELLS/PYMCA

Swapping the pavement for the boards.
A breakdancer gets his mind and his head in
a whirl at a New York City venue, 1987.

De la calle a la pista de baile. Un bailarín de
breakdance enfoca el mundo desde una nueva
perspectiva en una sala de Nueva York, 1987.

Dalla strada alla pista da ballo. Un ballerino
di breakdance fa turbinare il corpo e la mente
in un ritrovo di New York, 1987.

A skateboarder takes off from the bottom of a chute on the south coast of England, Southsea, 1989.

Un joven con monopatín se lanza desde una pista de *skateboard* en la costa meridional de Inglaterra, Southsea, 1989.

Un giovane su skateboard decolla dall'estremità di una pista, Southsea, costa meridionale dell'Inghilterra, 1989.

Students stretch their muscles and warm up for a dance class at Flagball School of Arts, North Carolina, 1986. Six years after the Alan Parker film *Fame*, many young people still had their sights firmly set on careers in entertainment.

Estiramientos y calentamiento en una clase de danza en la Flagball School of Arts, Carolina del Norte, Estados Unidos, 1986. Seis años después de la película de Alan Parker *Fama*, muchos jóvenes seguían decididos a dedicarse al espectáculo.

Esercizi di stiramento e preriscaldamento prima di una lezione di ballo presso la Flagball School of Arts, North Carolina, 1986. Sei anni dopo *Fame*, il film di Alan Parker, molti giovani nutrivano ancora la ferma determinazione di fare carriera nel mondo dello spettacolo.

For the hip, on the hip: the ubiquitous Sony Walkman. A young Japanese woman steps out, 1982.

Con la moda a cuestas: el ubicuo *walkman* de Sony. Una joven japonesa a paso ligero por las calles de su ciudad, 1982.

Un accessorio al passo con i tempi: l'onnipresente walkman della Sony. Una giovane giapponese a passeggio, 1982.

NAOKI OKAMOTO/BLACK STAR/COLORIFIC!

Music on the move, USA 1985. It lacked the portability of the Walkman, but the ghetto-blaster allowed others to share your taste in music and its young owner the chance to annoy passing fuddy-duddies.

Con la música a cuestas, Estados Unidos, 1985. No era portátil como el *walkman*, pero el radiocasete permitía compartir los gustos musicales propios con los demás y daba a los jóvenes la oportunidad de molestar a los transeúntes más conservadores.

Musica in movimento, Stati Uniti, 1985. Gli enormi radioregistratori, i cosiddetti ghetto-blaster, non erano comodi da trasportare come il walkman, ma presentavano il vantaggio di far condividere agli altri i gusti musicali dei loro possessori, i quali, tra l'altro, avevano così anche l'occasione di infastidire i matusa di passaggio.

JOHN REARDON/THE OBSERVER/HULTON|ARCHIVE

The message of the wall reads: 'I want some drugs.' But the boy in the frame has to be content with a cigarette, an empty foil container and a dab of glue. Such was the glamour of the drug culture in the 1980s.

En la pared se lee: "Quiero drogas". Pero el chico de la fotografía tiene que conformarse con un cigarrillo, un trozo de papel de aluminio y un poco de pegamento: así de glamurosa era la cultura de las drogas en los años ochenta.

La scritta sulla parete recita: "Voglio droga". Ma il ragazzo della foto deve arrangiarsi con una sigaretta, un sacchetto di alluminio vuoto e un poco di colla. Ecco l'incanto della cultura della droga degli anni Ottanta.

Panic in Needle Park? Aftermath of a heavy smack session, Alphabet City, New York. Penalties for possession and dealing were increased in the 1980s, but the scoring and the ODs continued.

¿Pánico en el "Parque de las agujas"? No, las consecuencias de una fuerte dosis de heroína en Alphabet City, Nueva York. Las penas por posesión y tráfico de drogas se endurecieron en los años ochenta, pero el consumo y las víctimas de sobredosis no disminuyeron.

Panico a Needle Park? Conseguenze dell'abuso di roba, Alphabet City, Stato di New York. Negli anni Ottanta furono aumentate le pene per il possesso e lo spaccio di droga, ma il consumo e le overdosi non diminuirono.

GABE KIRCHHEIMER/BLACK STAR/COLORIFIC!

It started as a revival of the spirit of Woodstock, but the first Rainbow Gatherings of the 1980s soon developed into a world-wide movement, with camps in Europe as well as on the Washington–Oregon border, 1989 (above).

Todo empezó como un renacer del espíritu del festival de Woodstock, pero los primeros encuentros denominados Rainbow Gatherings, celebrados en los años ochenta, pronto dieron paso a un movimiento de escala mundial, con campamentos en Europa y en la frontera entre Washington y Oregón, 1989 (arriba).

I primi raduni Rainbow degli anni Ottanta cominciarono come un risveglio dello spirito di Woodstock, ma ben presto divennero un movimento di livello mondiale, con accampamenti sia in Europa che qui, in qualche punto al confine tra gli stati di Washington e Oregon, 1989 (in alto).

A scene of domestic tranquillity inside one of the tents at the same Rainbow Gathering, Washington–Oregon, USA, 1989.

Una escena de paz doméstica en el interior de una tienda de la misma Rainbow Gathering de la página anterior, frontera entre Washington y Oregón, Estados Unidos, 1989.

Una tranquilla scena domestica all'interno di una delle tende dello stesso raduno Rainbow, al confine tra gli stati di Washington e Oregon, Stati Uniti, 1989.

GABE KIRCHHEIMER/BLACK STAR/COLORIFIC!

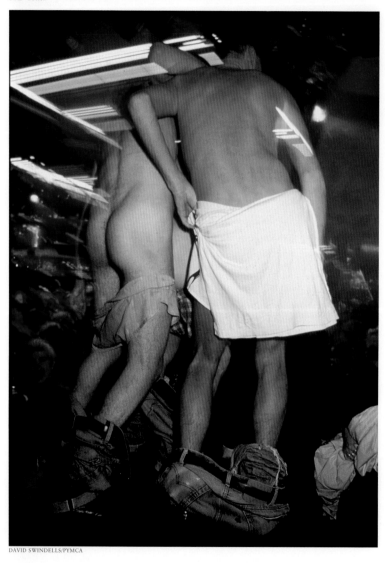

Drop 'em, boys –
lads show their
credentials at 'Disco-
Teque' in the spring
of 1988.

Pantalones fuera.
Unos muchachos
enseñan su currículo
en Disco-Teque,
primavera de 1988.

Nudi, nudi! Dei
giovani esibiscono le
proprie credenziali
alla "Disco-Teque",
primavera del 1988.

DAVID SWINDELLS/PYMCA

Not quite slaves to the rave. By the late Eighties the 'lad culture' had
infiltrated the scene and started to transform it. It wasn't a pretty sight.
(Above) Spectrum, 1989.

No tan esclavos de las *raves*. A finales de los años ochenta, la "cultura
del macho" se había infiltrado en la escena y empezó a transformarla.
No era un espectáculo demasiado agradable. (Arriba) Spectrum, 1989.

Non proprio schiavi della frenesia. Verso la fine degli anni Ottanta la
"lad culture", il binomio macho-alcol, fece il suo ingresso nella vita
notturna, iniziando a trasformarla. Come spettacolo non era un gran
che. (In alto) Spectrum, 1989.

When Ibiza was just another island… A drunken British tourist dead to the world outside a burger bar, 4 September 1984.

Cuando Ibiza era una isla cualquiera… Un turista británico completamente borracho y dormido como un troco delante de una hamburguesería, 4 de septiembre 1984.

Quando Ibiza diventò un'appendice del Regno Unito… Un turista britannico ubriaco e dimentico del mondo davanti ad un bar, 4 settembre 1984.

JOHN REARDON/THE OBSERVER/HULTON|ARCHIVE

Riding the rave.
Dancers work up
a heavy sweat at
Pacha I, Ibiza, 1989.
By now the rave
scene was a part of
the island's culture.

En plena fiesta.
Dos asistentes a la
discoteca Pachá I
de Ibiza en 1989,
bailando y sudando
sin parar. El *rave* ya
formaba parte de la
cultura isleña.

In piena frenesia.
Ballerini grondanti
sudore al Pacha I,
Ibiza, 1989. Ormai
il rave era parte
integrante della
cultura dell'isola.

DAVID SWINDELLS/PYMCA

City of London
policemen question
a would-be
anarchist near the
Stock Exchange,
27 September 1984.
A 'Stop the City'
demonstration
was expected.

Policías de la
City de Londres
interrogando a un
pseudo anarquista
cerca de la Bolsa,
27 de septiembre
de 1984.
Estaba prevista una
manifestación con
el lema "Stop the
City".

Dei poliziotti di
Londra interrogano
un aspirante
anarchico vicino alla
Borsa, 27 settembre
1984. Nell'aria c'era
una dimostrazione
per bloccare
l'attività della City.

PA

A boot camp guard fails to pick on someone his own size, Forsyth, Georgia, 1987.
'Boot camp' was the popular name for the unpopular alternative incarceration facilities
pioneered in the States.

Un guardia de un centro de menores se enfrenta a un interno que no le llega ni al hombro,
en Forsyth, Georgia, 1987. Estados Unidos fue pionero en la introducción de estos
impopulares centros penitenciarios alternativos, denominados popularmente "boot camps".

Un sorvegliante di un campo di detenzione se la prende con chi è più piccolo di lui,
Forsyth, Georgia, 1987. "Boot camp", campi degli stivali, erano popolarmente chiamate
le impopolari strutture carcerarie alternative introdotte per la prima volta negli Stati Uniti.

ROBIN NELSON/BLACK STAR/COLORIFIC!

Life became more complicated for professional and amateur sociologists in the 1980s. In the old days, skinheads (above) were almost unanimously condemned as brutish, neo-Fascists. By 1989 'skinhead' was a style, not a personality.

Los sociólogos profesionales y aficionados tuvieron las cosas más difíciles en los años ochenta. Hasta entonces, los *skinheads* o cabezas rapadas (arriba) se definían casi unánimemente como jóvenes violentos y neofascistas. Pero en 1989 ya era una categoría estética más que ideológica.

Gli anni Ottanta complicarono la vita ai sociologi professionisti e a quelli dilettanti. Ai vecchi tempi, gli skinhead (in alto) erano quasi unanimemente censurati come brutali neofascisti. Nel 1989, "skinhead" indicava uno stile, non una personalità.

For some, however, the old ways remained. (Right) A skinhead at a British Movement rally, Notting Hill, London, 2 June 1980.

En algunos casos, sin embargo, seguían vigentes las viejas reglas. (Derecha) Un *skinhead* en ua manifestación de la extrema derecha británica, Notting Hill, Londres, 2 de junio de 1980.

Qualcuno, però, rimase fedele ai propri principi. (A destra) uno skinhead ad una manifestazione dell'organizzazione britannica di estrema destra British Movement, Notting Hill, Londra, 2 giugno 1980.

STUART NICOL/EVENING STANDARD/HULTON|ARCHIVE

10. Sport
Deportes
Sport

Ben Johnson slips into the lead during the men's 100 metres final at the Seoul Olympics, 1988. Johnson finished first, but was stripped of his gold medal two days later for using an illegal substance.

Ben Johnson colocándose en cabeza durante la final masculina de los 100 metros en los Juegos Olímpicos de Seúl, 1988. Johnson acabó en primer lugar, pero fue despojado de la medalla de oro dos días después por el consumo de una sustancia ilegal.

Ben Johnson scivola in testa durante la finale dei 100 metri maschili alle Olimpiadi di Seoul, 1988. Johnson arrivò primo, ma la medaglia d'oro gli fu ritirata due giorni dopo perché aveva fatto uso di una sostanza illecita.

10. Sport
Deportes
Sport

Never before had sport attracted so many followers, received so much publicity or generated so much wealth. Nor had it ever experienced such tragedy and drama as it did in the 1980s. Almost a hundred years earlier, the Baron de Coubertin had inaugurated the modern Olympic movement and stated the Olympic ideal. In the 1988 Olympics at Seoul what mattered was not taking illegal substances. Drugs cost Ben Johnson of Canada a gold medal; they later cost several athletes their careers.

Football was hit by appalling tragedies. In May 1985, fifty-six football fans were killed in a fire. Less than three weeks later thirty-nine fans were crushed to death in the crumbling Heysel Stadium, Brussels. Worse followed. On 15 April 1989, ninety-five Liverpool fans died during an FA Cup semi-final.

But sport continued on its way. France, West Germany and Argentina dominated international football. The USA and the Soviet Union swept the field in athletics. West Germany grabbed tennis glory through Boris Becker and Steffi Graf. India and Australia took cricket's World Cup. There was something for everyone.

El deporte nunca había tenido tantos seguidores, recibido tanta publicidad ni generado tanta riqueza. Ni había vivido tragedias y dramas como los de los años ochenta. Casi cien años atrás, el barón de Coubertin había inaugurado los juegos olímpicos modernos y expresado el ideal olímpico. Pero en los Juegos Olímpicos de Seúl de 1988 lo más importante resultó ser no haber tomado sustancias ilegales: las drogas le costaron al atleta canadiense Ben Johnson una medalla de oro y posteriormente arruinarían las carreras de varios atletas.

El fútbol sufrió terribles tragedias. En mayo de 1985, 56 aficionados murieron en un incendio. Apenas tres semanas después, 39 hinchas más murieron aplastados cuando se vino abajo parte del estadio Heysel de Bruselas. Y todavía quedaba lo peor. El 15 de abril de 1989, 95 seguidores del Liverpool murieron durante una semifinal de la copa inglesa.

Pero el deporte siguió su camino. Francia, Alemania Occidental y Argentina dominaban el fútbol internacional. Estados Unidos y la Unión Soviética arrasaron en el campo del atletismo. Alemania Occidental triunfó en el tenis con Boris Becker y Steffi Graf. India y Australia se llevaron la copa del mundo de *cricket*. En fin, hubo algo para todos.

Lo sport non aveva mai avuto tanti sostenitori né ricevuto tanta pubblicità e creato tanta ricchezza. Non era mai stato neppure al centro di tante tragedie e drammi come negli anni Ottanta. Quasi cento anni prima, il barone de Coubertin aveva dato vita al movimento delle moderne Olimpiadi, risuscitando l'ideale olimpico. Alle Olimpiadi di Seoul del 1988, l'argomento del giorno fu il doping. Le droghe costarono una medaglia d'oro al canadese Ben Johnson e, in seguito, posero fine alla carriera di molti atleti.

Il calcio fu sconvolto da terribili tragedie. Nel maggio del 1985, cinquantasei tifosi morirono in un incendio. Meno di tre settimane dopo, trentanove tifosi rimasero uccisi dal crollo di una parete dello stadio Heysel di Bruxelles. Seguirono tragedie ancora peggiori. Il 15 aprile 1989, novantacinque tifosi del Liverpool morirono durante una semifinale del campionato britannico.

Ma lo sport continuò per la sua strada. La Francia, la Germania Occidentale e l'Argentina dominavano il calcio internazionale. Gli Stati Uniti e l'Unione Sovietica facevano man bassa di medaglie nel campo dell'atletica. La Germania Occidentale conobbe la gloria del tennis grazie a Boris Becker e a Steffi Graf. L'India e l'Australia vinsero il campionato mondiale di cricket. Ciascuno ebbe la sua parte.

PETER GINTER/BLACK STAR/COLORIFIC!

(Opposite) Carl Lewis in the blocks at the World Championships, Rome, Italy, 1987. For much of the 1980s Lewis was the fastest man in the world. (Above) Florence Griffith Joyner stretches those muscles, 1989.

(Página anterior) Carl Lewis en el taco de salida del campeonato del mundo, Roma, Italia, 1987. Durante buena parte de los años ochenta, Lewis fue el hombre más rápido del mundo. (Arriba) Florence Griffith Joyner haciendo estiramientos, 1989.

(Pagina a fianco) Carl Lewis ai blocchi di partenza durante i campionati mondiali di Roma, Italia, 1987. Lewis rimase l'uomo più veloce del mondo durante quasi tutto il decennio. (In alto) Florence Griffith Joyner stira i muscoli, 1989.

Sebastian Coe
establishes a new
world record for
the mile – 3 minutes
31.26 seconds,
Zurich,
21 August 1981.

Sebastian Coe
bate un nuevo
récord mundial en
la milla: 3 minutos,
31,26 segundos,
Zúrich, 21 de agosto
de 1981.

Sebastian Coe
stabilisce un nuovo
record mondiale
sul miglio, 3 minuti
e 31,26 secondi,
Zurigo, 21 agosto
1981.

Steve Ovett (388) struggles in the final of the 1500 metres, Los Angeles Olympics, 1984. Cram (362) took the silver medal while Coe took the gold.

Steve Ovett (388) lucha por ganar la final de los 1.500 metros, Juegos Olímpicos de Los Ángeles, 1984. Cram (362) se llevó la medalla de plata y Coe, el oro.

Steve Ovett (388) lotta nella finale dei 1500 metri alle Olimpiadi di Los Angeles, 1984. Cram (362) vinse la medaglia d'argento, mentre Coe vinse l'oro.

Björn Borg sinks
to his knees after
winning his fifth
successive men's
singles championship
at Wimbledon,
July 1980.

Björn Borg cae de
rodillas tras ganar
su quinto título
individual
consecutivo en
el torneo de
Wimbledon,
julio de 1980.

Björn Borg cade in
ginocchio dopo aver
vinto il torneo di
Wimbledon per la
quinta volta, luglio
1980.

John McEnroe in a pit of despair after losing a point in the Wimbledon Championships, July 1989. His days of triumph in the early 1980s were over. There were new stars abroad.

John McEnroe, desesperado tras perder un punto en el torneo de Wimbledon, julio de 1989. Sus días de gloria de principios de los años ochenta ya habían tocado a su fin. Era el turno de las nuevas estrellas.

John McEnroe si dispera dopo aver perso un punto al torneo di Wimbledon, luglio 1989. I suoi giorni di gloria degli inizi degli anni Ottanta erano ormai finiti. Nuove stelle brillavano all'orizzonte.

Boris Becker at full stretch during the French
Open Championships, Paris, 1987. It was a
lean year for Becker.

Boris Becker dándolo todo de sí durante el
torneo de Roland-Garros, París, 1987. Fue
un mal año para Becker.

Boris Becker teso come un elastico agli
Open francesi, Parigi, 1987. Per lui fu
un anno magro.

Forehand. Steffi
Graf on her way
to winning the
Australian Open,
Melbourne,
January 1989.

Golpe de derecha.
Steffi Graf a punto
de ganar el Open
de Australia,
Melbourne,
enero de 1989.

Colpo di dritto.
Steffi Graf sul punto
di vincere gli
Open australiani,
Melbourne, gennaio
1989.

CLIVE BRUNSKILL/ALLSPORT

Backhand? Ivan Lendl, Wimbledon, July 1989, the year in which he also won the Australian Open for the first time.

¿Revés? Ivan Lendl en Wimbledon, en julio de 1989, el año en que también ganó por primera vez el Open de Australia.

Rovescio? Ivan Lendl, Wimbledon, luglio 1989. Lo stesso anno in cui vinse anche gli Open australiani per la prima volta.

ALLSPORT

Leon Spinks,
Heavyweight
Champion of
the World, picks
on a flyweight,
Miami Airport,
18 April 1988.

Leon Spinks,
campeón del
mundo de los
pesos pesados,
levantando a
un peso mosca,
aeropuerto de
Miami, 18 de abril
de 1988.

Leon Spinks,
campione del
mondo dei pesi
massimi, solleva
un peso mosca
all'aeroporto di
Miami, 18 aprile
1988.

TIM CHAPMAN/LIAISON AGENCY

MICHAEL BAYTOFF/BLACK STAR/COLORIFIC!

Mike Tyson with promoter Don King (in private breeze), 1988. These were the glory years for 'Iron Mike', who had world title wins over James 'Bonecrusher' Smith, Tyrell Smith, Larry Holmes, Michael Spinks, Frank Bruno and Carl Williams.

Mike Tyson y su promotor Don King (con la melena al viento), 1988. Fueron años gloriosos para *Iron Mike*, quien ganó varios títulos mundiales tras enfrentarse con James *Quebrantahuesos* Smith, Tyrell Smith, Larry Holmes, Michael Spinks, Frank Bruno y Carl Williams.

Mike Tyson con l'organizzatore Don King (con i capelli al vento), 1988. Erano gli anni gloriosi di "Iron Mike", che aveva battuto James "Bonecrusher" Smith, Tyrell Smith, Larry Holmes, Michael Spinks, Frank Bruno e Carl Williams in altrettanti incontri per il titolo mondiale.

First round KO. Mike Tyson is restrained by the referee after putting Michael Spinks on the canvas, Atlantic City, 27 June 1988.

K. O. en el primer *round*. El árbitro retiene a Mike Tyson después de que este tirara a Michael Spinks a la lona, Atlantic City, 27 de junio de 1988.

KO al primo round. L'arbitro trattiene a stento Mike Tyson, che ha appena messo al tappeto Michael Spinks. Atlantic City, 27 giugno 1988.

You lookin' at me? Mike Tyson poses during training in January 1986. Training was his least favourite part of the fight game.

¿Y tú qué miras? Mike Tyson posa durante un entrenamiento en enero de 1986. El entrenamiento era lo que menos le gustaba del boxeo. Prefería el combate.

Che hai da guardare? Mike Tyson in posa durante un allenamento nel gennaio del 1986. L'allenamento era la parte che meno gli piaceva. Preferiva combattere.

ROBERT DIBUE/ALLSPORT

In the bank. US
basketball star
Michael Jordan
in his classic 'Air
Jordan' leap for a
Nike advertisement,
1987.

Encestando.
La estrella del
baloncesto
estadounidense
Michael Jordan
con su clásico salto
"Air Jordan", para
un anuncio de Nike,
1987.

Di sponda. La
star del basket
statunitense
Michael Jordan nel
suo classico "balzo
aereo" per una
pubblicità della
Nike, 1987.

In the basket. Magic
Johnson of the
Los Angeles Lakers
goes for a basket
during the 1989
championships.

Canasta. Magic
Johnson, del equipo
Los Angeles Lakers,
a punto de encestar
durante el
campeonato
de 1989.

Canestro. Magic
Johnson dei Los
Angeles Lakers
sul punto di fare
canestro ai
campionati
del 1989.

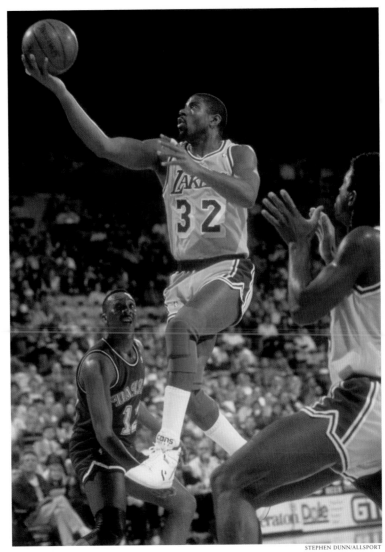

STEPHEN DUNN/ALLSPORT

Beam me up, Stocky. Chelle Stock of the USA at the women's team gymnastics final, Seoul Olympics, 21 September 1988.

Una sonrisita… La estadounidense Chelle Stock en la final de gimnasia femenina por equipos, Juegos Olímpicos de Seúl, 21 de septiembre 1988.

Fammi un bel sorriso, Stocky. La statunitense Chelle Stock alla finale di ginnastica femminile delle Olimpiadi di Seoul, 21 settembre 1988.

Another perfect 10? Nadia Comaneci of Romania on her way to gold at the Moscow Olympics, 19 July 1980, the year she excelled.

¿Otro 10? La rumana Nadia Comaneci a punto de ganar el oro en los Juegos Olímpicos de Moscú, 19 de julio de 1980, un año en el que tuvo un rendimiento excelente.

Un altro 10? La rumena Nadia Comaneci sulla strada dell'oro alle Olimpiadi di Mosca, 19 luglio 1989.

TONY DUFFY/ALLSPORT

MIKE POWELL/ALLSPORT

Horses and riders clear not the highest but perhaps the hardest jump in the Grand National – Becher's Brook, Aintree, Liverpool, April 1983. It was originally a water jump, named after Captain Martin Becher.

Caballos y jinetes saltan no el obstáculo más alto, sino seguramente el más difícil, en el torneo Grand National, Becher's Brook, Aintree, Liverpool, abril de 1983. En su origen era un salto sobre agua, bautizado en honor del capitán Martin Becher.

Cavalli e fantini superano un ostacolo, non il più alto ma forse il più difficile del Grand National, Becher's Brook, Aintree, Liverpool, aprile 1983. In origine era una riviera battezzata con il nome del capitano Martin Becher.

BOB MARTIN/ALLSPORT

Captain Becher took a tumble from his horse, Conrad, in 1839. (Above)
Riders and horses (including the grey Dark Ivy, centre) follow in the
captain's footsteps during the 1987 Grand National.

El capitán Becher se había caído de su caballo, Conrad, en 1839. (Arriba)
Los jinetes y caballos de la fotografía (incluido el caballo gris *Dark Ivy*,
centro) siguen sus pasos durante el Grand National de 1987.

Il capitano Becher cadde da cavallo a Conrad nel 1839. (In alto) Fantini
e cavalli (tra cui il cavallo grigio Dark Ivy) seguono le orme del capitano
durante il Grand National del 1987.

Mauricio Gugelmin of Brazil takes to the air
after shunting Nigel Mansell's Ferrari during
the French Grand Prix, 9 July 1989.

El brasileño Mauricio Gugelmin salta por
los aires después de chocar con el Ferrari
de Nigel Mansell durante el Grand Prix
de Francia, 9 de julio de 1989.

Il brasiliano Mauricio Gugelmin vola in
aria dopo aver tamponato la Ferrari di
Nigel Mansell al Gran Premio di Francia,
9 luglio 1989.

DAVID CANNON/ALLSPORT

French captain Michel Platini wheels away in triumph after his goal against Brazil in the World Cup quarter-final at the Jalisco Stadium, Guadalajara, Mexico, 21 June 1986. France won 4-3 on penalties.

El capitán del equipo francés Michel Platini corre por el césped para celebrar la victoria tras su gol contra Brasil en los cuartos de final del Mundial, en el estadio de Jalisco, Guadalajara, México, 21 de junio de 1986. Francia ganó 4 a 3 en la tanda de penaltis.

Un trionfante Michel Platini, capitano della squadra francese, dopo aver segnato un gol contro il Brasile nei quarti di finale dei Mondiali allo stadio Jalisco di Guadalajara, Messico, 21 giugno 1986. La Francia vinse ai rigori per 4 a 3.

ALLSPORT UK

Ruud Gullit (left) and Gerald Vanenburg take off on a lap of honour
after Holland beat the Soviet Union 2-0 in the European
Championship Final, Olympic Stadium, Munich, 25 June 1988.

Ruud Gullit (izquierda) y Gerald Vanenburg dan la vuelta de honor
después de que Holanda derrotara a la URSS por 2 a 0 en la final del
campeonato europeo, Estadio Olímpico de Múnich, 25 de junio
de 1988.

Giro d'onore di Ruud Gullit (a sinistra) e Gerald Vanenburg dopo la
vittoria dell'Olanda sull'Unione Sovietica per 2 a 0 alla finale degli
Europei, stadio olimpico di Monaco, 25 giugno 1988.

ALLSPORT UK

The camera cannot lie; the ref couldn't see. Diego Maradona and the Hand of God slip the ball past Peter Shilton, World Cup quarter-final, Mexico City, 22 June 1986. English hearts were broken.

La cámara no miente, aunque el árbitro no lo viera. La "mano de Dios" de Diego Armando Maradona le quita la pelota a Peter Shilton, en los cuartos de final del Mundial de México, 22 de junio de 1986. A los ingleses se les partió el corazón.

La telecamera non mente; l'arbitro non l'ha visto. La "mano di Dio" di Diego Maradona spinge la palla in rete oltre Peter Shilton ai quarti di finale dei Mondiali di Città del Messico, 22 giugno 1986. Uno spettacolo che spezzò i cuori inglesi.

Three weeks earlier, the Knees of God were most cruelly fouled. Maradona in an earlier World Cup game, June 1986.

Tres semanas antes, se había cometido una cruel falta contra las rodillas de "Dios". Maradona, en un partido anterior del Mundial de junio de 1986.

Tre settimane prima, le "ginocchia di Dio" di Maradona avevano subito un duro fallo in una precedente partita del campionato, giugno 1986.

EAMONN McCABE/THE OBSERVER/HULTON|ARCHIVE

One of the darkest days in the history of sport: football fans are crushed after
a wall collapses at the Heysel Stadium, Brussels, 29 May 1985, just before the
start of the European Cup Final.

Uno de los días más sombríos de la historia del deporte: aficionados al fútbol
aplastados después de que se viniera abajo un muro del estadio Heysel, Bruselas,
el 29 de mayo de 1985, justo antes de la final de la Copa de Europa.

Una delle giornate più tragiche della storia dello sport: poco prima dell'inizio
della finale degli Europei, dei tifosi vengono calpestati in seguito al crollo di
una parete dello stadio Heysel di Bruxelles, 29 maggio 1985.

NICK DIDLICK/REUTERS/HULTON|ARCHIVE

Trouble began when fighting broke out between supporters of Liverpool and Juventus. By the time it was over, thirty-nine lay dead and more than 400 injured. (Above) A harrowing image of the aftermath.

Todo empezó cuando se inició una pelea entre los aficionados del Liverpool y de la Juventus. El resultado de la refriega fueron 39 víctimas mortales y más de 400 heridos. (Arriba) Una imagen desgarradora de las consecuencias de la tragedia.

Gli incidenti cominciarono dopo una rissa tra i tifosi del Liverpool e quelli della Juventus. Il bilancio fu di trentanove morti e più di 400 feriti. (In alto) Una straziante immagine della tragedia.

11. Children
Los más pequeños
Bambini

Two young children photographed in south-west China, 1989. Whatever benefits it had brought, forty years of Communism had apparently failed to alter traditional gender stereotyping.

Dos niños pequeños fotografiados en el sudoeste de China, 1989. A pesar de los posibles beneficios aportados por el sistema, cuarenta años de comunismo aparentemente no habían conseguido modificar los estereotipos tradicionales de género.

Due bambini fotografati nel sudovest della Cina, 1989. Quarant'anni di comunismo possono anche aver presentato dei vantaggi, ma non sono riusciti ad alterare la tradizionale separazione tra i ruoli sessuali.

11. Children
Los más pequeños
Bambini

The 1960s had invented the teenager; the 1970s had seen the full flowering of 'youth'. It was time for children to reappear on the world stage. In the 1980s they did so in a series of tragedies whose themes were war, famine and exploitation. One 14-year-old from Mozambique declared: 'I have never seen peace. I don't know what peace is. I have never lived in freedom.' He spoke for millions of African children.

All over the world there were stories of gangs of children who lived by begging on the streets, stealing the hubcaps of cars, prostituting themselves, scrabbling for food on garbage heaps. Television viewers flinched as they saw how children lived in the Sudan, in Beirut, in Romanian orphanages, in military camps, in the slums of South America.

In more comfortable lands, traders set out their stalls for children. There was a spate of children's films, from *ET* to *Flash Gordon* and *Superman*. Toyshops bulged with a mixture of the old hand-made toys and new big money-spinners that were battery operated and made of plastic; bookshops were filled with 'game books', fantasy adventure stories. But the most popular new toy was the computer.

En los años sesenta se inventó el "adolescente" y en los setenta se asistió al pleno desarrollo de "los jóvenes". Había llegado el momento de que los niños reaparecieran en el escenario mundial. Y lo hicieron en los años ochenta con una serie de tragedias derivadas de la guerra, el hambre y la explotación. Como declaró un niño de 14 años natural de Mozambique: "Nunca he conocido la paz. No sé qué es la paz. Nunca he vivido en libertad". Y hablaba en nombre de millones de niños africanos.

En todo el mundo se descubrieron historias de bandas infantiles que vivían mendicando en las calles, robando los tapacubos de los coches, prostituyéndose o escarbando en las montañas de basura en busca de comida. Los televidentes se estremecieron al ver cómo vivían los niños en el Sudán, en Beirut, en los orfanatos rumanos, en los campos militares o en los barrios bajos de Sudamérica.

En los países ricos, los comercios salieron en busca de la clientela infantil. Hubo un aluvión de películas infantiles, de *E. T. el extraterrestre* a *Flash Gordon* y *Superman*. Las tiendas de juguetes estaban repletas de una combinación de juguetes antiguos de fabricación artesanal y nuevos artículos de plástico a pilas de ventas millonarias; las librerías se llenaron de "libros juego", cuentos de aventuras y fantásticos. Pero el nuevo juguete más popular fue el ordenador.

I teenager furono un'invenzione degli anni Sessanta; il decennio successivo vide il pieno fiorire dei "giovani". I tempi erano ormai maturi perché i bambini riapparissero sulla scena mondiale. Lo fecero negli anni Ottanta, con una serie di tragedie legate alla guerra, alla carestia e allo sfruttamento. Un quattordicenne mozambicano dichiarò: "Non ho mai visto la pace. Non so cosa sia la pace. Non ho mai vissuto la libertà". Parlava in nome di milioni di bambini africani.

Il mondo era pieno di storie di bande di bambini che sopravvivevano mendicando per le strade, rubando i coprimozzo dalle ruote delle automobili, prostituendosi, frugando nei cumuli di spazzatura alla ricerca di cibo. I telespettatori trasalivano alla vista del modo in cui i bambini vivevano in Sudan, a Beirut, negli orfanotrofi rumeni, in campi militari, nelle baraccopoli sudamericane.

Nei paesi ricchi il mercato andava a caccia di piccoli consumatori. Un diluvio di film per bambini invadeva gli schermi, da *E.T.* a *Flash Gordon* passando per *Superman*. I negozi di giocattoli traboccavano di un miscuglio di vecchi gingilli fatti a mano e di nuove miniere d'oro fabbricate in plastica ed azionate a batteria; le librerie erano piene di "libri giocattolo" che narravano avventure fantastiche. Ma dei nuovi giocattoli, il più popolare era il computer.

The hug of humanity. Pope John Paul II embraces a child AIDS victim, 1987. The picture helped de-stigmatise sufferers from the disease.

El abrazo de la humanidad. El papa Juan Pablo II abraza a un niño víctima del sida, 1987. Esta fotografía contribuyó a desestigmatizar a los afectados por la enfermedad.

Un gesto umano. Il papa Giovanni Paolo II abbraccia un bambino malato di AIDS, 1987. L'immagine contribuì alla lotta contro l'emarginazione dei malati di AIDS.

Just say no. Nancy Reagan, First Lady of the United States, at an anti-drugs demonstration, Washington, DC, May 1988.

"Di no". Nancy Reagan, primera dama de Estados Unidos, en una manifestación contra la droga, Washington, mayo de 1988.

No alla droga. Nancy Reagan, moglie del presidente degli Stati Uniti, ad una manifestazione antidroga a Washington, maggio 1988.

DENNIS BRACK/BLACK STAR/COLORIFIC!

J KUUS/SIPA PRESS

Francie, a 13-year-old suffering from Hutchinson-Gilford syndrome, April 1986. The condition leads to premature ageing, which affects the heart and arteries. Few victims survive beyond the age of 30.

Francie, de 13 años, afectado por el síndrome Hutchinson-Gilford, abril de 1986. Esta enfermedad causa el envejecimiento prematuro, que ataca el corazón y las arterias. Pocos afectados viven más de 30 años.

Francie, una tredicenne con sindrome di Hutchinson-Gilford, aprile 1986. Questa malattia conduce all'invecchiamento precoce, con conseguenze sul cuore e le arterie. Raramente chi ne patisce supera i 30 anni di vita.

H K OWEN/BLACK STAR/COLORIFIC!

Isolated from germs, 6-year-old David undergoes tests at the clinical research centre of the Texas Children's Hospital, September 1980. David was a victim of severe combined immune deficiency, a hereditary disease affecting only males.

Aislado de los microbios, David, de seis años de edad, se somete a unas pruebas en el centro de investigaciones clínicas del hospital infantil de Texas, septiembre de 1980. David sufría inmunodeficencia combinada grave, una enfermedad hereditaria que afecta solo al sexo masculino.

Isolato dai germi, David, di 6 anni, si sottopone a degli esami presso il centro di ricerche cliniche del Texas Children's Hospital, settembre 1980. David pativa di immunodeficienza combinata grave, una malattia ereditaria che colpisce solo i maschi.

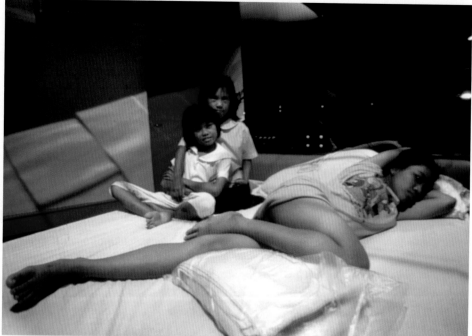

CHRISTOPH HENNING/FOTOARCHIV/COLORIFIC!

A brief respite from work, a moment back in childhood. Child prostitutes at the Queensland Lodge, Manila, the Philippines, 1989. Such abuse was centuries old. The awakening of the world's conscience was a new phenomenon.

Un breve descanso del trabajo, un momento para volver a la infancia. Prostitutas infantiles en Queensland Lodge, Manila, Filipinas, 1989. Estos abusos se habían cometido durante siglos: el despertar de la conciencia mundial era un fenómeno nuevo.

Una breve pausa durante il lavoro. Bambini si prostituiscono al Queensland Lodge, Manila, Filippine, 1989. Tali abusi erano vecchi di secoli. Il risveglio della coscienza mondiale fu invece un fenomeno nuovo.

Thai bar girls compete in a condom-blowing contest as part of the Thailand Fights AIDS campaign held in the red light district of Bangkok, 6 September 1989. One of the signs reads: 'We need your help & co-operation.' Not enough has arrived – yet.

Niñas empleadas en bares tailandeses durante un concurso de inflar preservativos, un acto de la campaña contra el sida en Tailandia, en el barrio con más prostitución de Bangkok, 6 de septiembre de 1989. Uno de los carteles dice: "Necesitamos tu ayuda y cooperación". Todavía no les ha llegado suficiente.

Impiegate di bar tailandesi partecipano ad una gara di gonfiamento di preservativi nel quadro della campagna tailandese di lotta contro l'AIDS tenutasi nel quartiere a luci rosse di Bangkok, 6 settembre 1989. Uno dei cartelli recita: "Abbiamo bisogno del vostro aiuto e della vostra cooperazione". A tutt'oggi, né l'uno né l'altra sono stati sufficienti.

JIM HOLLANDER/REUTERS/HULTON ARCHIVE

Other distractions.
Palestinian
schoolgirls file past
Israeli soldiers who
are frisking adult
Palestinians on the
Gaza Strip,
November 1986.

Otras distracciones.
Niñas palestinas de
camino al colegio
pasan junto a unos
soldados israelíes
que cachean a
adultos palestinos,
franja de Gaza,
noviembre de 1986.

Altre distrazioni.
Scolare palestinesi
sfilano accanto a
soldati israeliani che
perquisiscono degli
adulti nella striscia
di Gaza, novembre
1986.

Life returns to normality on the streets of El Salvador, Central
America, 1982. A troop of guerrilla fighters had just passed through
the town of Sanbertoco when these children set off for school.

Vuelta a la normalidad en las calles de El Salvador, Centroamérica,
1982. Cuando estas niñas se dirigían a la escuela, una banda de
guerrilleros acababan de atravesar la población de Sanbertoco.

Ritorno alla normalità nelle strade di El Salvador, America Centrale,
1982. Questi bambini si recano a scuola poco dopo il passaggio di
un reparto di guerriglieri attraverso la cittadina di Sanbertoco.

Children take to the streets of Beirut at the height of the fighting, March 1985. There were plenty of 12-year-old soldiers in the Lebanon at this time, with 'heavy-duty lace-up boots, skinhead haircuts and Kalashnikovs', reported one surgeon.

Los niños se echan a las calles de Beirut en el punto culminante de los enfrentamientos, marzo de 1985. En aquella época había muchos soldados de 12 años en el Líbano, con "botas militares, cabezas rapadas y fusiles Kalashnikov", según declaró un cirujano.

I bambini scendono in strada a Beirut all'apice dei combattimenti, marzo 1985. A quei tempi abbondavano in Libano i soldati dodicenni con "stivaloni, teste rasate in stile skinhead e kalashnikov", come riferì un chirurgo.

A young recruit to the Ku Klux Klan gives a Nazi salute. In some places old obscenities lingered on into the 1980s.

Un joven recluta del Ku Klux Klan realizando el saludo nazi. En algunos lugares, se mantuvieron antiguas obscenidades como esta en los años ochenta .

Una giovane recluta del Ku Klux Klan fa il saluto nazista. In alcuni luoghi, vecchie oscenità si trascinavano ancora fino agli anni Ottanta.

GAVIN WATSON/PYMCA

In a world of his own, a boy patrols the outskirts of West Wycombe, Buckinghamshire, keeping it safe for democracy, 1981. Happily, the weapon is a toy and nothing worse than unemployment threatened his town.

Absorto en su mundo, un niño patrulla por las afueras de West Wycombe, Buckinghamshire, con el fin de mantener el respeto por la democracia, 1981. Afortunadamente, el arma es de juguete y su población no sufría más amenazas que el desempleo.

Perduto nel suo mondo. Un ragazzino pattuglia la periferia di West Wycombe, Buckinghamshire, difendendo la democrazia, 1981. Per fortuna l'arma è un giocattolo e l'unica cosa che minaccia la cittadina è la disoccupazione.

CHRISTOPHER MORRIS/BLACK STAR/COLORIFIC!

The greatest craze of the 1980s. A young skateboarder, wisely wearing helmet, and elbow and knee pads (don't leave home without them), displays concentration and balance, May 1981.

La afición más popular de los años ochenta. Un joven con monopatín, y la prudencia de llevar casco, coderas y rodilleras (no salgan de casa sin ellos), demuestra concentración y equilibrio, mayo de 1981.

La gran voga degli anni Ottanta. Un giovanissimo fa sfoggio di concentrazione ed equilibrio con skateboard indossando saggiamente casco, coprigomito e ginocchiere ("Non uscire di casa senza portarteli dietro!"), maggio 1981.

Ten-year-old Terry O'Neill masters Rubik's Cube at the British Toy and Hobby Fair, Earl's Court, London, 2 February 1981.

Terry O'Neill, de diez años de edad, demostrando su dominio del cubo de Rubik en la feria de juguetes y tiempo libre británica, Earl's Court, Londres, 2 febrero de 1981.

Terry O'Neill, 10 anni, domina il Cubo di Rubik alla fiera dei giocattoli e del tempo libero di Earl's Court, Londra, 2 febbraio 1981.

SIMON NORFOLK/PYMCA

Please sir…? A hungry pupil hopes for a second sausage in the queue for school dinners, Wales, 1989. For an increasing number of children, the school dinner was their one hot meal of the day.

Por favor, señor… Una niña hambrienta pide otra salchicha en la cola del comedor del colegio, Gales, 1989. Cada vez había más niños que comían caliente una sola vez al día: en el comedor del colegio.

Un altro po', per favore… Una scolara affamata, in coda alla mensa, spera di ricevere un'altra salsiccia, Galles, 1989. Per un numero sempre maggiore di bambini, il pranzo della scuola costituiva l'unico pasto caldo della giornata.

CHRISTOPHER MORRIS/BLACK STAR/COLORIFIC!

A boy helps himself at a soup kitchen, New York City, September 1989. Research into child health revealed that malnutrition was not confined to the Third World in the 1980s.

Un niño se sirve sopa en un comedor de beneficencia, Nueva York, septiembre de 1989. Los estudios sobre salud infantil revelaron que en los años ochenta la desnutrición no se limitaba al Tercer Mundo.

Self-service in una mensa per poveri, New York, settembre 1989. Negli anni Ottanta, le ricerche sulla salute infantile rivelarono che la malnutrizione non era solo un problema del Terzo Mondo.

The delights of the VDU. For many children the computer was a
modern magic lantern, opening up new worlds, revealing new
wonders and ultimately leading to new employment opportunities.

La magia del monitor. Para muchos niños, el ordenador fue como
una linterna mágica que abría paso a nuevos mundos maravillosos y
desconocidos, y en último término a nuevas oportunidades de empleo.

La magia dello schermo. Per molti bambini il computer fu una
moderna lanterna magica che apriva loro nuovi mondi, rivelava
nuove meraviglie e, in seguito, avrebbe condotto a nuove
opportunità lavorative.

For others, computers were thousands of miles and millions of pesos away. A young coal vendor hugs his doll in a shanty town, somewhere in El Salvador 1988.

Para otros, los ordenadores estaban a una distancia de miles de kilómetros y millones de pesos. Una vendedora de carbón con una muñeca en El Salvador, 1988.

Per altri, i computer restavano a migliaia di chilometri e milioni di *pesos* di distanza. Una giovane venditrice di carbone coccola la sua bambola in una baraccopoli, da qualche parte in El Salvador, 1988.

12. All human life
Cosas de la vida
Fatti della vita

An AIDS victim being massaged by Irene Smith, a hospice
therapist, in San Francisco, California, 1986. Two weeks
later, the poor man died.

Una víctima del sida recibe un masaje de Irene Smith, fisioterapeuta
de una residencia para enfermos sin recursos, en San Francisco,
California, 1986. El pobre hombre murió dos semanas después.

Irene Smith, terapeuta di un ricovero di San Francisco, California,
massaggia un malato di AIDS, 1986. Il poveretto morì due
settimane dopo.

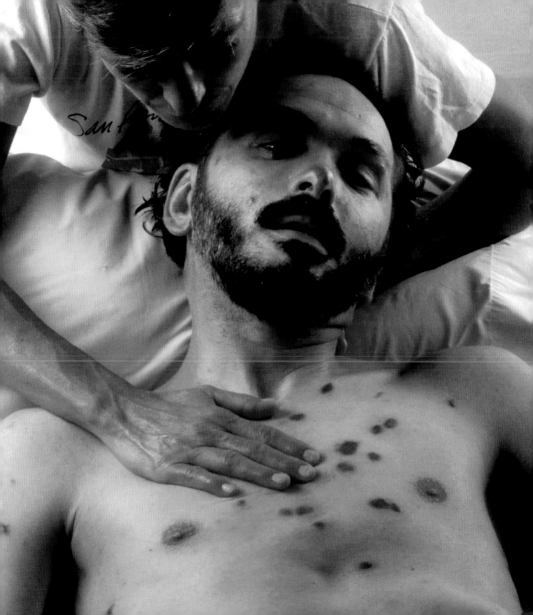

12. All human life
Cosas de la vida
Fatti della vita

To and fro swung the pendulum of progress and reaction. The first black Miss America was crowned in September 1983. Just over a year later Margie Velma Barfield became the first woman to be executed in the USA for more than twenty-two years. Crack cocaine appeared. Ben and Jerry became ice-cream millionaires. After scandals involving Jimmy Swaggart ('moral transgression') and Jim Bakker (fraud), two of America's most popular TV ministers faded from the screen.

Elsewhere, the Turin Shroud was shown to have been a low-tech medieval creation, and *The Hitler Diaries* to have been the product of a fertile imagination but not that of the Führer. The matador Francisco Rivera died after being gored in the thigh: the offending bull's mother was promptly killed. In England the Yorkshire Ripper was convicted of murdering thirteen women.

More people married, more divorced. There were more holidays. For the fortunate minority, the world opened up like a giant playground. For the majority, there were brief respites from want and misery, when hope bloomed like a flower in the desert.

La década transcurrió a golpe de péndulo, oscilando entre avances y retrocesos. En septiembre de 1983 se eligió a la primera Miss América de raza negra. Justo un año más tarde murió Margie Velma Barfield, la primera mujer ejecutada en Estados Unidos en 22 años. En el mundo de las drogas, hizo su aparición el *crack*. La empresa Ben and Jerry se convirtió en un gran imperio del helado. Después de sendos escándalos, dos de los más populares predicadores televisivos de Estados Unidos, Jimmy Swaggart y Jim Bakker, desaparecieron de las pantallas del país, acusados de "pecado moral" y fraude, respectivamente.

Por otra parte, el sudario de Turín resultó ser un artefacto medieval de baja tecnología y se demostró que los diarios de Hitler eran fruto de una fértil imaginación, pero no precisamente la del *Führer*. El torero Francisco Rivera murió tras sufrir una cornada en el muslo: la madre del toro en cuestión fue sacrificada de inmediato. En Inglaterra, el asesino conocido como el "destripador de Yorkshire" fue declarado culpable de asesinar a trece mujeres.

A lo largo de la década, hubo más bodas y divorcios que nunca. También se disfrutó de más vacaciones. Para una minoría afortunada, el mundo se estaba convirtiendo en un inmenso parque de atracciones. Pero para la mayoría, la vida estaba llena de miseria y carencias que tan solo podían olvidarse en las raras ocasiones en que la esperanza florecía como una solitaria rosa del desierto.

Il pendolo oscillava avanti e indietro tra il progresso e la reazione. La prima Miss America di colore fu incoronata nel settembre del 1983. Un anno dopo Margie Velma Barfield fu la prima donna giustiziata negli Stati Uniti dopo oltre ventidue anni. Il crack fece la sua comparsa. Gli americani Ben e Jerry diventarono milionari vendendo gelati. Coinvolti in scandali, due tra i predicatori televisivi più popolari d'America, Jimmy Swaggart ("comportamento immorale") e Jim Bakker (frode) scomparvero dai teleschermi.

In altre latitudini, si dimostrò che la Sacra Sindone non era altro che una rudimentale creazione medievale e che i Diari di Hitler erano stati il frutto di una fertile immaginazione, non però quella del führer. Il torero Francisco Rivera morì per un'incornata alla coscia, e la madre del toro criminale fu uccisa immediatamente. In Inghilterra, lo Squartatore dello Yorkshire fu dichiarato colpevole dell'assassinio di tredici donne.

La gente si sposava di più e divorziava di più. Le vacanze aumentarono. Per una fortunata minoranza, il mondo si aprì come un immenso campo da gioco. Per la maggior parte delle persone, invece, vi erano solo brevi momenti di tregua tra il bisogno e la miseria, quando la speranza sbocciava come un fiore nel deserto.

On 29 April 1988,
the top of this
Boeing 737 was
torn off 20,000
feet above Hawaii.
It landed safely
and only one
passenger died.

El 29 de abril de
1988, la parte
superior de este
Boeing 737 se
desprendió a 6.000
metros de altitud
sobre Hawai.
El piloto consiguió
aterrizar y solo
murió un pasajero.

Il 29 aprile 1988,
la parte superiore
di questo Boeing
737 fu strappata
via a 6000 metri di
altitudine al disopra
delle Hawaii.
L'apparecchio riuscì
ad atterrare al sicuro
e solo un passeggero
perse la vita.

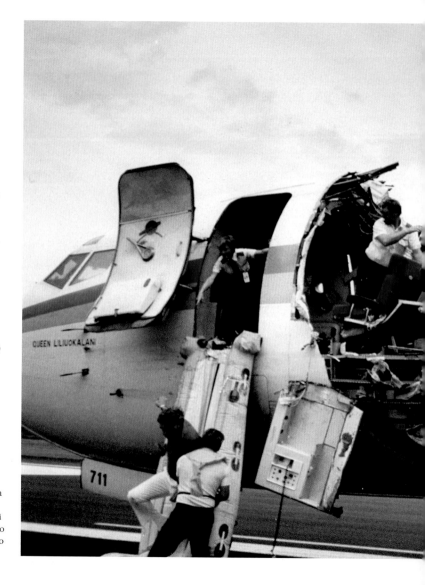

'88 4 29

NASA/LIAISON AGENCY

(Above) The doomed crew of the fatally flawed *Challenger* space mission, 11 November 1985. Nine weeks later all died when *Challenger* exploded after take-off (left).

(Arriba) La malograda tripulación de la tristemente defectuosa nave espacial *Challenger*, el 11 de noviembre de 1985. Nueve semanas después todos murieron al producirse la explosión de la nave tras el despegue (izquierda).

(In alto) Lo sfortunato equipaggio della missione spaziale *Challenger*, destinata alla catastrofe, 11 novembre 1985. Morirono tutti nove settimane dopo, quando il *Challenger* esplose poco dopo il decollo (a sinistra).

A penitent atones for sins committed during Lent, the Philippines, April 1981. Such voluntary acts of public shame have now become tourist attractions.

Una penitente expía los pecados cometidos durante la Cuaresma, Filipinas, abril de 1981. Estos actos voluntarios de castigo autoinfligido y público se han convertido en atracciones turísticas.

Una penitente espia i peccati commessi durante la quaresima, Filippine, aprile 1981. Questi atti di penitenza pubblica sono ormai diventati attrazioni turistiche.

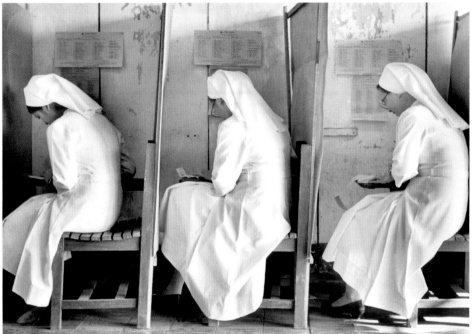

Nuns registering their votes in the presidential contest between
Ferdinand Marcos and Corazon Aquino, widow of the former
Opposition leader, the Philippines, 7 February 1986.

Monjas votando en las elecciones presidenciales. Los candidatos
eran Ferdinand Marcos y Corazón Aquino, viuda del antiguo líder
de la oposición, Filipinas, 7 de febrero de 1986.

Delle suore votano alle presidenziali in cui si sarebbe deciso tra
Ferdinand Marcos e Corazón Aquino, vedova dell'ex leader
dell'opposizione, Filippine, 7 febbraio 1986.

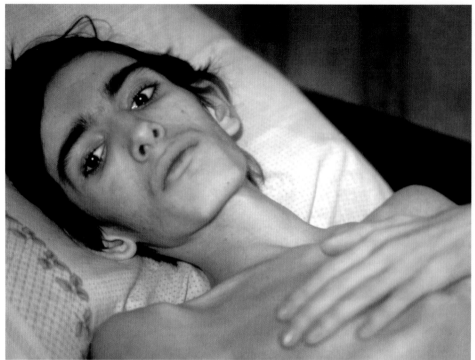

IGOR COSTIN/STERN/BLACK STAR/COLORIFIC!

One of the tens of thousands of victims of the Chernobyl disaster, Ukraine,
26 April 1986. An unauthorised test by engineers caused an explosion that
started a horrendous fire in the nuclear plant.

Una de las decenas de miles de víctimas de la catástrofe de Chernóbil, Ucrania,
26 de abril de 1986. Unos ingenieros efectuaron una prueba no autorizada que
provocó una explosión y un terrible incendio en la central nuclear.

Una delle decine di migliaia di vittime del disastro di Chernobyl, Ucraina,
26 aprile 1986. L'esplosione fu causata da un esperimento che alcuni ingegneri
eseguirono senza autorizzazione, e generò un terribile incendio nella centrale
nucleare.

JAY ULALL/STERN/BLACK STAR/COLORIFIC!

A relation holds a photograph of one of more than 2,500 people killed when toxic gas leaked from the Union Carbide plant in Bhopal, India, 13 December 1984. It was only one of a series of leaks. Union Carbide later paid out $470 million in compensation.

Una mujer con una fotografía de un pariente, una de las más de 2.500 personas que murieron a causa de la emanación de gas tóxico de la fábrica de Union Carbide en Bhopal, India, el 13 de diciembre 1984. Fue solo una de varias fugas. Union Carbide pagó posteriormente 470 millones de dólares en concepto de indemnizaciones.

Una parente mostra la fotografia di una delle oltre 2.500 persone che persero la vita a causa della fuoriuscita di gas tossico dallo stabilimento della Union Carbide a Bhopal, India, 13 dicembre 1984. Fu solo una delle tante fuoriuscite di gas. In seguito la Union Carbide pagò 470 milioni di dollari a titolo di compensazione.

CEM AKKAN/ANZENBERGER/COLORIFIC!

Whirling dervishes perform their traditional trance-inducing dance at the House of Mevlevi, Istanbul, Turkey. The dancers spin round sixty times a minute for periods of up to half an hour.

Derviches interpretando su danza tradicional, inductora de un estado de trance, en la Casa de Mevlevi, Estambul, Turquía. Los bailarines dan sesenta vueltas por minuto durante períodos de hasta media hora.

Turbinio di dervisci durante la tradizionale danza che induce all'estasi mistica nella Casa di Mevlevi a Istanbul, Turchia. Per circa mezz'ora, i ballerini ruotano su sé stessi sessanta volte al minuto.

FAUSTO GIACCONE/ANZENBERGER/COLORIFIC!

Mennonites on the march in Paraguay in the 1980s. Many Anabaptist followers in the footsteps of their 16th-century founder Menno Simons left Europe for South America in the 1950s, and established religious colonies in Paraguay.

Menonitas caminando por Paraguay en los años ochenta. Muchos anabaptistas seguidores de Mennón Simons, fundador de esta doctrina en el siglo XVI, abandonaron Europa para instalarse en Sudamérica en los años cincuenta y fundaron colonias religiosas en Paraguay.

Mennoniti in marcia in Paraguay negli anni Ottanta. Molti seguaci dell'anabattista del XVI secolo Menno Simons lasciarono l'Europa alla volta del Sudamerica negli anni Cinquanta e fondarono colonie religiose in Paraguay.

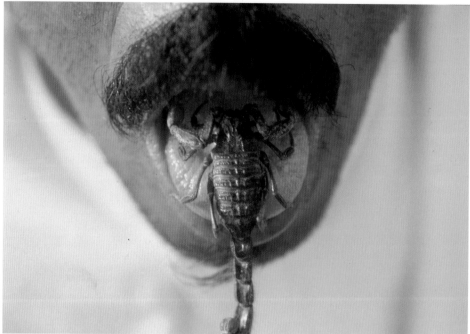

BRUNO HADJIH/ANZENBERGER/COLORIFIC!

At one with nature… A scorpion worshipper admits the object of
his reverence to the temple of his mouth, Morocco. No one should
doubt that considerable faith is involved here.

En comunión con la naturaleza… Un adorador del escorpión
admite el objeto de su veneración en el templo de su boca,
Marruecos. Nadie duda de que su fe era realmente inquebrantable.

Tutt'uno con la natura… Un adoratore di scorpioni accoglie
l'oggetto della sua venerazione nel tempio della bocca, Marocco.
Indubbiamente, ciò comporta una buona dose di fede.

At more than one
with nature…
A contestant in the
1985 Bee Beard
Competition. Let's
hope he was the
winner.

En absoluta
comunión con la
naturaleza…
Un participante en el
concurso de "barbas
de abejas" de 1985.
Esperemos que por
lo menos fuera el
ganador de la
competición.

Osmosi totale con
la natura… Un
partecipante ad
un concorso per
la barba d'api del
1985. C'è da sperare
che sia risultato
vincitore.

CHRISTOPHER MORRIS/BLACK STAR/COLORIFIC!

RICHARD HOWARD/BLACK STAR/COLORIFIC!

A pair of mice used in genetic research at the Jackson Laboratory, Maine, 1983. Laboratories that used rodents were usually safe from animal rights activists. Those that used cats or dogs, or anything larger, weren't.

Un par de ratones utilizados en pruebas de investigación genética en el laboratorio Jackson, Maine, 1983. Los laboratorios que investigaban con roedores no solían recibir las quejas de los defensores de los derechos de los animales. No era el caso de los que utilizaban gatos, perros o animales más grandes.

Due topi utilizzati per la ricerca genetica presso il Jackson Laboratory, Maine, 1983. In genere, i laboratori che usavano roditori erano al sicuro dagli attivisti per i diritti degli animali. Quelli che usavano gatti o cani, invece, non lo erano affatto.

MICHAEL MONTFORT/VISAGES/COLORIFIC!

The harpoon that cures. Fish become aquatic 'guinea pigs' as they are used for research into the properties of acupuncture. The surprising outcome would seem to be how little the needles have affected the fishes' balance.

El arpón curativo. Peces cumpliendo la función de cobayas acuáticas en un estudio sobre las propiedades de la acupuntura. Lo sorprendente es lo poco que afectan las agujas al equilibrio de los peces.

L'arpione curativo. I pesci divennero cavie acquatiche usate per le ricerche sulle proprietà dell'agopuntura. Per quanto possa sembrare sorprendente, pare che gli aghi non abbiano influito molto sul senso dell'equilibrio dei pesci.

CHARLES MASON/BLACK STAR/COLORIFIC!

One of a series of photographs recording the harvesting of reindeer antlers in Alaska, 1989. By the late 1980s the antlers had become more valuable than the meat, providing much-needed income to a remote state of the USA.

Fotografía de un reportaje sobre la "recolección" de astas de reno en Alaska, 1989. A finales de los años ochenta, los cuernos ya eran más apreciados que la carne de este animal y aportaban unos ingresos muy necesarios al remoto estado de Estados Unidos.

Una fotografia tratta da una serie sulla raccolta di corna di renna in Alaska, 1989. Verso la fine degli anni Ottanta le corna divennero più preziose della carne, creando una fonte di introiti di cui il remoto Stato degli USA aveva urgente bisogno.

JEFFREY ROTMAN /BLACK STAR/COLORIFIC!

A young warrior from one of Africa's smallest tribes prepares to deliver the *coup de grâce* to a hippopotamus, Lake Turkana, Kenya. The tribe, who both worshipped and hunted hippos, numbered only thirty-seven in the 1980s.

Un joven guerrero de una de las tribus más pequeñas de África se prepara para asestar el golpe de gracia a un hipopótamo, lago Turkana, Kenia. La tribu, que adoraba a los hipopótamos, pero también los cazaba, tenía entonces apenas 37 miembros.

Un giovane guerriero appartenente ad una delle più piccole tribù africane si prepara ad assestare il colpo di grazia ad un ippopotamo, Lago Turkana, Kenya. La tribù venerava e allo stesso tempo cacciava gli ippopotami, e negli anni Ottanta contava solo trentasette membri.

CLAUDE CHARLIER/BLACK STAR/COLORIFIC!

Putting it on… A contestant in the *Guinness Book of Records* World's Heaviest Man Contest, Japan, April 1986. To beat the all-time record, held by Robert Earl Hughes, the contestant had to weigh in at over 485 kilograms.

Engordar… Un participante del concurso del hombre más gordo del mundo del *Libro Guinness de los récords*, Japón, abril de 1986. Para batir el récord mundial, en posesión de Robert Earl Hughes, el concursante debía pesar más de 485 kilogramos.

Un chilo sull'altro… Un partecipante al concorso per l'uomo più pesante del mondo organizzato per il Guinness dei primati, Giappone, aprile 1986. Per poter battere il record mondiale detenuto da Robert Earl Hughes, il partecipante doveva pesare più di 485 chilogrammi.

ROBIN NELSON/BLACK STAR/COLORIFIC!

Taking it off… Two aspiring weight losers appear to be in good heart (they'd need to be) at this Diet Disco in the Landmark Hotel, Durham, North Carolina, May 1989. Obesity was reaching epidemic proportions in the Unites States.

Adelgazar… Dos personas a régimen y, al parecer, con la moral muy alta (la necesitaban) en una discoteca dietética del hotel Landmark, Durham, Carolina del Norte, mayo de 1989. La obesidad alcanzó proporciones epidémicas en Estados Unidos

Qualche chiletto in meno… Due aspiranti a dimagrire ridono di cuore (non gli restava altro da fare) alla discoteca dietetica del Landmark Hotel di Durham, North Carolina, maggio 1989. Negli Stati Uniti l'obesità stava ormai assumendo le proporzioni di un'epidemia.

Bronze beauty. Catherine Wilke (standing) passes shelves of sunbathers on the Mediterranean island of Capri, August 1980.

Belleza bronceada. Catherine Wilke (de pie) pasa junto a unas camillas superpuestas llenas de mujeres al sol, en la isla mediterránea de Capri, agosto de 1980.

Bellezza di bronzo. Catherine Wilke (in piedi) davanti a bagnanti sovrapposte a prendere il sole sull'isola mediterranea di Capri, agosto 1980.

SLIM AARONS/HULTON ARCHIVE

Golden greed.
Fortune hunters
digging for gold in
the province of Para,
Brazil, 1985.

La fiebre del oro.
Cazadores de
fortunas escarban
en busca de oro en
la provincia de Para,
Brasil, 1985.

Corsa all'oro.
Cacciatori di fortuna
scavano alla ricerca
di oro nello stato del
Pará, Brasile, 1985.

CLAUS MEYER/BLACK STAR/COLORIFIC!

MANFRED HORVATH/ANZENBERGER/COLORIFIC!

Hungarians, with maybe one or two Czech mates, play chess by the pool at the Szechenyi-Bad spa, Budapest. It was the Indian summer of Communist control in Eastern Europe.

Ciudadanos húngaros, quizá junto a un par de checos, juegan al ajedrez al lado de la piscina del balneario de Szechenyi-Bad, Budapest. Era el epílogo del control comunista sobre Europa del Este.

Degli ungheresi, e forse un paio di colleghi cechi, giocano a scacchi presso la piscina della stazione termale di Szechenyi-Bad, Budapest. Era l'estate di San Martino del controllo comunista sull'Europa orientale.

JOSEF POLLEROSS/ANZENBERGER/COLORIFIC!

Two truckers take a break from the road and concentrate on the video game consoles at Truckworld, Ohio. Hopefully, the machines make it quite clear exactly where the coin is to be inserted to start the machine.

Dos camioneros se distraen con unos videojuegos mientras descansan de la carretera, Truckworld, Ohio, Estados Unidos. Esperemos que las máquinas indicaran claramente dónde había que introducir las monedas.

Due camionisti si concentrano su un videogioco durante una pausa lungo il cammino a Truckworld, Ohio. C'è da sperare che le macchine indichino chiaramente dove vada inserita la moneta per giocare.

GERRY GROPP/COLORIFIC!

The big match, US-style… Safety helmets at rakish angles, teams compete in a game of motorised croquet, Black Rock Desert, near Gerlach, Nevada, 1987. The setting is ideal for the game – a level surface, plenty of space and no rain.

Partidazo, al estilo americano… Partido de *croquet* motorizado en el desierto de Black Rock, próximo a Gerlach, Nevada, 1987. El terreno es ideal para el juego: superficie lisa, mucho espacio y sin amenaza de lluvias.

Partita all'americana… Con gli elmetti di sicurezza sulle ventitré, le squadre partecipano ad una partita di croquet motorizzato nel deserto di Black Rock vicino a Gerlach, Nevada, 1987. Il posto è ideale per questo gioco: superficie piana, abbondanza di spazio e niente pioggia.

BILL EPPRIDGE/COLORIFIC!

The big match, Indian-style… Nellie the Striker (newly transferred from Madras United for a record fee of three rupees per pound) bears down on goal in a game of elephant football. Why doesn't the goalie nip out and whip the ball away from her tusks?

Partidazo, al estilo indio… La delantera Nellie la elefanta (recién transferida del Madras United por una suma récord de tres rupias por kilo) chuta a gol en un partido de fútbol elefantiano. ¿Por qué será que el portero no avanza para birlarle la pelota a su contrincante de entre los colmillos?

Partita all'indiana… l'attaccante Nellie (venduta da poco dal Madras United per la somma record di tre rupie alla libbra) carica in direzione della porta durante una partita di calcio con elefanti. Perché mai il portiere non esce a toglierle il pallone dalle zanne?

Index

gettyimages

Over 70 million images and 30,000 hours of film footage are held by the various collections owned by Getty Images. These cover a vast number of subjects from the earliest photojournalism to current press photography, sports, social history and geography. Getty Images' conceptual imagery is renowned amongst creative end users.

www.gettyimages.com

Más de 70 millones de imágenes y 30.000 horas de secuencias filmadas forman parte de las muchas colecciones que pertenecen a Getty Images. Éstas cubren un vasto número de temas desde los principios del periodismo fotográfico hasta la actual fotografía de prensa, deportes, historia social y geografía. Las imágenes conceptuales de Getty Images tienen renombre entre sus creativos consumidores.

www.gettyimages.com

Le varie collezioni di proprietà della Getty Images comprendono oltre 70 milioni di immagini e 30.000 ore di filmati che abbracciano un ampio numero di soggetti: il giornalismo fotografico dalle origini ai giorni nostri, lo sport, la storia sociale e la geografia. Le immagini concettuali della Getty images sono rinomate fra gli utenti finali del settore creativo.

www.gettyimages.com

Acknowledgements

The picture editor is grateful to the following individuals and agencies or collections with which they are associated for their assistance with this book:

Christopher Angeloglou, Julius Domoney, David Leverton and Sally Ryall (Colorific!); Anh Stack and Michelle Hernandez (Black Star); Rosa Di Salvo, Richard Ellis, Bob Hechler, Hilary Johnston, Robert Pepper, Eric Smalkin (Liaison Agency); Rob Harborne, Lee Martin and Matthew Stevens (Allsport); Mitch Blank, Kathy Lavelle, Eric Rachlis, Peter Rohowsky and Arlete Santos (Hulton|Archive, New York); Antonia Hille, Sarah Kemp and Alex Linghorn (Hulton|Archive, London); Jake Cunningham (PYMCA); Martin Stephens and Milica Timotic (PA News); Gul Duzyol and Jocelyne Manfredi (Sipa Press); Judith Caul and Tony Mancini (*The Guardian*); Jim Docherty and Marianne Lassen (S.I.N.); Simon Kenton (Idols); and to Sara Green and Stephanie Hudson for their kind assistance in New York and London respectively.